FRANZ **KEMPF**

Thinking on Paper

1955 – 2002

SASHA GRISHIN | ADAM DUTKIEWICZ | ROBERT SMITH

This book is sincerely dedicated to the authors, in gratitude for their faith and interest in my work; to the photographers, whose work I admire; to all those who have been supportive of my work – collectors, dealers and friends; to Arts SA, The Myer Family Foundation, and Wakefield Press, who have made this publication possible; and to my wife, Tamar, with love.

Franz Kempf

Wakefield Press
17 Rundle Street
Kent Town
South Australia 5067

First published 2002

First published to coincide with the *Franz Kempf: Thinking on Paper, 1955–2002* exhibition held at the Flinders University Art Museum from 13 September to 31 October 2002.

Designed by Dean Lahn,
Lahn Stafford Design
Printed and bound by Hyde Park Press

Photography
Peter Ayres, page 9
Colin Ballantyne, page 5
Mick Bradley, pages 6, 7
David Wilson, pages 18–63

Cover: *In the Beginning*, 2002
Title page: *Blessing of the Moon*, 1992

All dimensions are given as height by width with measurements in centimetres.

National Library of Australia
Cataloguing-in-publication entry

Grishin, Sasha.
Franz Kempf: thinking on paper
1955–2002.

ISBN 1 86254 592 8.

1. Kempf, Franz, 1926– . 2. Artists – Australia – Biography. I. Smith, Robert, 1928– . II. Dutkiewicz, Adam, 1956– . III. Title.

759.994

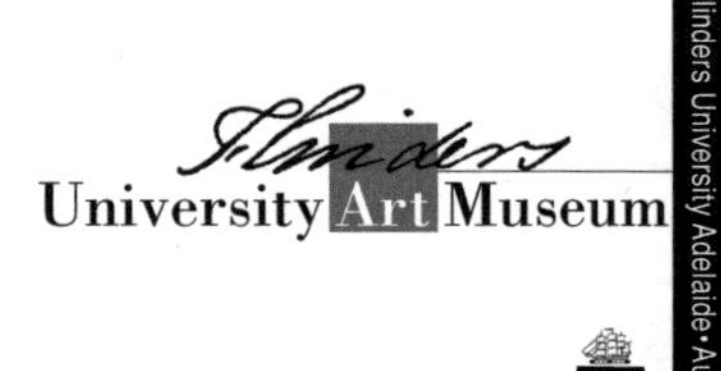

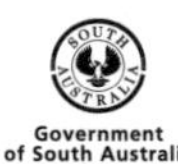

The production of this book has been assisted by the South Australian Government through Arts South Australia.

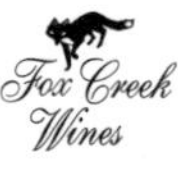

Wakefield Press thanks Fox Creek Wines and Arts South Australia for their support.

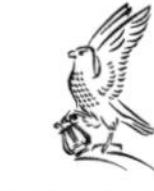

THE MYER FOUNDATION

FRANZ **KEMPF**

Thinking on Paper

1955 – 2002

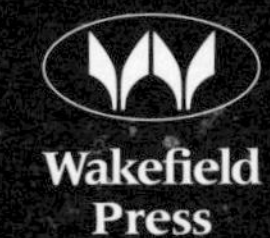

CONTENTS

FOREWORD

DAVID DOLAN

When invited to write a personal foreword to this volume, I wondered what I could say to add to the appreciations of Franz Kempf's art provided by Sasha Grishin, Robert Smith and Adam Dutkiewicz. I have had my say about his art in several journal articles dating from the time long ago when we were colleagues at the South Australian School of Art. So I will take as my starting point the truism that art is made by artists who are human beings.

While also acknowledging Kempf's work as a pioneering teacher, Sasha Grishin and Adam Dutkiewicz refer, in the learned essays that follow, to convictions, values, and commitments to the ethical, humanistic, and religious dimensions of art, and to the essentialist, mystical and elite aspects of Kempf's art practice.

Certainly, the high standards Kempf set as a teacher were important in developing a generation of younger artists who have since reached maturity. His combination of teaching and practice throughout the 1960s and 1970s when Australian art was in an exciting stage, means that he has a unique significance in our modern art history. But another aspect of his educational role, and his contribution to the social and intellectual climate of modern Australia, is his humanity and personality.

The artist is not just a channeller of stardust: the artist is a creature of flesh and blood and brain – in this case a twentieth-century Australian male working with the cultural traditions Australia has inherited and imported. Franz Kempf is not a wowser or an ascetic. He is not a cross between an old testament prophet, a plaster saint and a middle European intellectual who was freakishly delivered, via a cultural wormhole, to modern Australia. He is someone with whom to look at art, have an argument and a drink, hatch a plot, and share an anecdote. His friends know and love him for his sense of humour, his naughty streak, and his eccentricities. An artist without human qualities and foibles, one who does not share human weaknesses and temptations, could never produce art with the humanity and resonance of Kempf at his best.

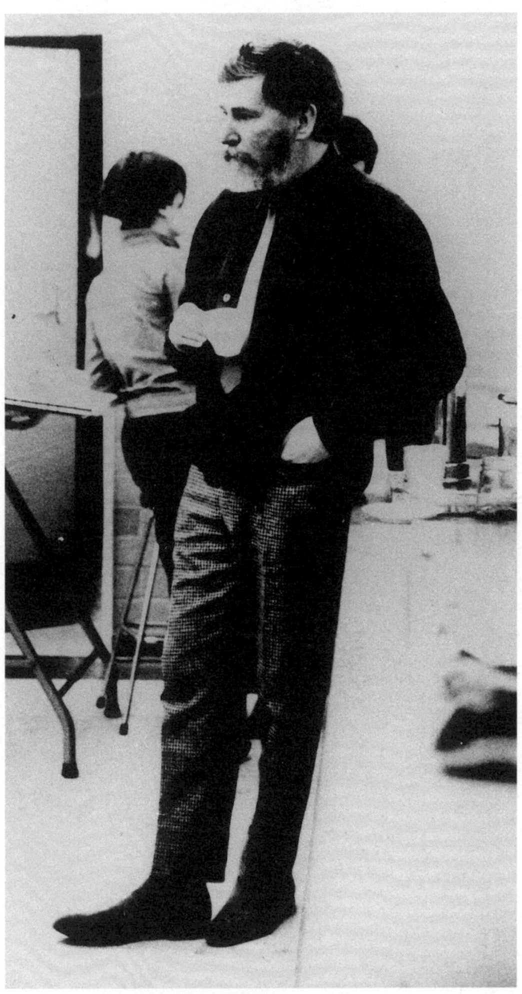

Franz Kempf, South Australian School of Art, 1972

WORKS ON PAPER

SASHA GRISHIN

Franz Kempf for many decades has appeared as an artist who has worked outside the conventions and fashions which prevailed in the art world in Australia. However, over the past few years his work has swung into fashion, and, in the contemporary context, it appears timely and concerned with the critical issues of the present. Perhaps it is the apocalyptic mood of the new century which has made a demand on art to engage with and confront the issues of this reality. An artist like Franz Kempf, now in his seventies, who has always been involved with these issues, is being recognised as a significant figure in the contemporary art movement.

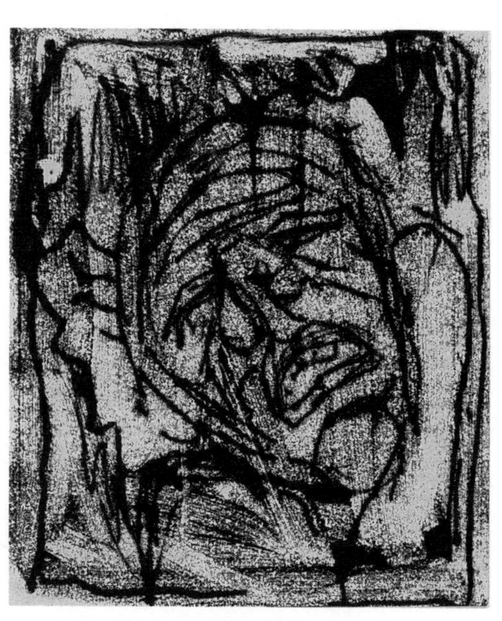

Pieta, 1998, monoprint, 22.5 x 19

As this collection of his works on paper shows, the main concerns in his art have remained relatively constant throughout his life. While he has always been committed to the ideal of the well-crafted, beautiful art object, Franz Kempf has also viewed the role of the artist as one who takes an ethical stance. Broadly speaking, Franz Kempf's stance is that of a humanist, one who celebrates the sanctity of all life, and one who finds a glimpse of the divine in nature and in all living things. Above all, he has been that most unfashionable of things in Australian art – a religious artist.

Franz Kempf's religious art is neither doctrinaire nor prescriptive. While some of his imagery is steeped within the traditions of his own Jewish faith, much of his thinking ranges freely over many religious conventions, drawing inspiration from the Koran and the New Testament among other sources.

There is a certain tyranny of recurring themes that runs throughout his work: memorials, Pietàs and images of war; passages and entrances, pantomimes and performers; and endless gardens and landscapes. Although the inquisitive biographer can legitimately discover autobiographical elements throughout his work, the imagery is rarely literal or descriptive. The image is conceived more as a metaphor where, like in a palimpsest, there are echoes of other realities.

An exegetic method is frequently employed when interpreting religious art. Here the image is not given a single narrative meaning, but several different meanings on a number of interconnected levels. This way of reading art was already known to early Christian commentators, for example, the fifth-century churchman John Cassian wrote:

History embraces the knowledge of things past and visible . . . to the allegorical belongs what follows, for what actually happened is said to have prefigured the form of some mystery . . . The anagogical rises from the spiritual mysteries even to still more sublime and sacred secrets of heaven . . . The tropological sense is the moral explanation . . . So the same Jerusalem can be taken in four senses: historically as the city of the Jews; allegorically as the Church of Christ; anagogically as the heavenly city of God . . . tropologically as the soul of man.

The images are multi-layered in Franz Kempf's work. It may be possible to perceive a narrative, a basic history, which may be anchored in a personal reality or in direct observation, but this invariably opens up further levels of interpretation. Allegory is frequently involved in his images with echoes from Scripture or history, ritual or tradition. The images also open up to spiritual and moral readings. So his image of a garden may refer to an actual garden or landscape, but then it could also be a reference to the Garden of Eden or the Garden of Gethsemane, or the eternal garden of the Tree of Life.

Franz Kempf's work thrives on this fluidity of interpretation and on its ability to weave a complex tapestry of meanings – some very personal and encoded, others universal and explicit. There is also something cyclical in his work – like a gathering of many facets of a single life-long theme. In images he has finished this year it is often possible to catch an echo of a theme that he may have tackled thirty or forty years ago. As he recently noted in a letter: 'somehow one is haunted by old twilight gods that refuse to go away, at times romantic, at others lurking in shadow ready to pounce'.

***Sasha Grishin** is an art historian, art critic and curator who studied art history at the universities of Melbourne, Moscow, London and Oxford. He is head of Art History at the Australian National University and has worked for many years as an art critic for the Australian and international press and been published extensively in contemporary and medieval art.*

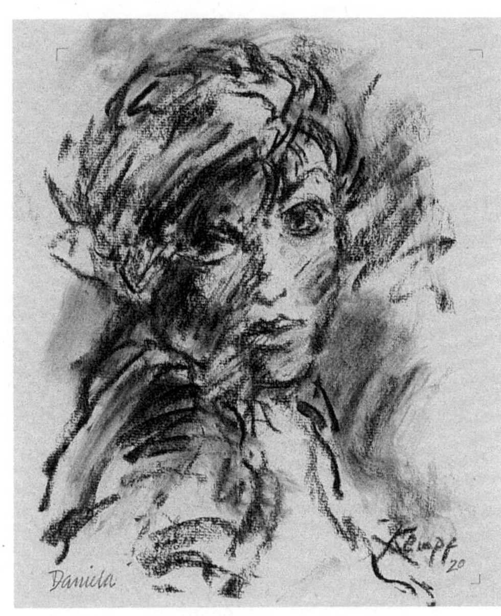

***Daniela**, 2000, charcoal drawing, 25 x 21*

OF BLUEPRINTS, CIRCLES AND STARDUST

ADAM DUTKIEWICZ

Franz Kempf won the Cornell Prize, the premier art prize offered through the Contemporary Art Society of South Australia from 1951 to 1965, towards the end of its life in 1964.[1] It was a sign of him having arrived in the Adelaide art world. Since then, he earned his reputation as a teacher at the South Australian School of Art, and for his emphasis on drawing as a thinking activity. He lectured in printmaking in the 1960s before establishing the Diploma of Printmaking in 1971.[2] In 1976 he produced *Contemporary Australian Printmaking*, the first comprehensive book on the subject in Australia.

Kempf's career has been charted by many, in catalogue essays, articles and books, in which there have been sizeable contributions by George Berger, Neville Weston, and Rosemary Brooks.[3] Ostensibly, this book begins where Weston's finished, in many respects completing the biography of his graphic work. But there is also a glimpse into his artistic life before he assumed his career as a teacher and artist in Adelaide, back to his earliest works in the 1940s and 50s in Melbourne, and his complementary life as a painter. It provides a neat set of parentheses to Weston's analysis, and spans fifty years of the artist's activity.

Such longevity in art these days is uncommon, and usually restricted to the elite, as only a few are sufficiently dedicated and capable of sustaining their careers without the formidable distractions of compromise and survival. It indicates Franz Kempf's firm commitment to his art and solid conviction in the values he pursues. As he puts it, 'Great works stand in their own right – irrespective of time, fashion or critics. Fashions change but art does not.'[4]

In examining Franz Kempf's *oeuvre*, one senses disquiet as his is an essentially European and Jewish sensibility trapped inside the boisterous and adolescent Australian culture. The spread of themes and the stylistic leaning of his work have formal and lyrical similarities with modern artistic models in Europe, especially Paul Cézanne, the early German expressionists, and the Italian post-war abstract painters Afro Basadella and Giuseppe Santomaso, whom he encountered in the early 1960s.[5]

These intertwined features do not conform to the common blueprint of Australian artistic careers in his era. The most famous and fashionable artists of that period, it seems, moved steadily towards a mature style that tended to reflect some iconic quality about the Australian bush, and thereafter departed little and ceased to experiment outside the parameters of that readily identifiable style. They eschewed the notable eclecticism of the European migrant artists of the immediate post-war years, who tended to become increasingly obscure as these legendary and quintessentially 'Australian' artists became giants.

And now, frequently, we see art critics such as John McDonald and Robert Nelson questioning the abilities and privileged status of some of these cultural icons, such as Brett Whiteley and Albert Tucker. And Franz Kempf, too, has quietly conducted his own discursive battle with the Antipodeans in his art, in his avoidance of impasto and overly loud visual pronouncements.

An interesting clue to the subtlety and complexity underpinning Franz Kempf's work is uncovered in the artist's notes. He mentions attending a lecture on Baroque music in 1987, while Artist in Residence at Mishkenot Sha'ananim, Yemin Moshe, Israel. In the discussion, the concept of the three circles in music was addressed by recitalist Laurette Goldberg. The first two circles are readily accessible: a matter of reading the score and getting the idea, then listening closely, but the third circle involves the penetration of the music's symbols.

For what is music? It is speech. But the composer speaks not in words but in symbols. He wants people to understand but knows that symbols communicate only to those who know how to interpret them. The composer describes a place, usually a secret place. People usually stand guard over a place like that and don't allow strangers to enter, but the composer is prepared to allow entry. If the listener has the strength and intelligence to pierce through to the centre of the music, it's a sign he or she resembles the artist to some extent. The listener is not an artist but is capable of understanding and therefore has permission to go inside. His entry will not disturb anything. The music's centre is not only a secret place but also a dangerous place. It's a world so beautiful, so pure, that if you go inside you have two problems. First, how can you bear all that beauty? And second, how will you get out and carry on living in the ordinary world?[6]

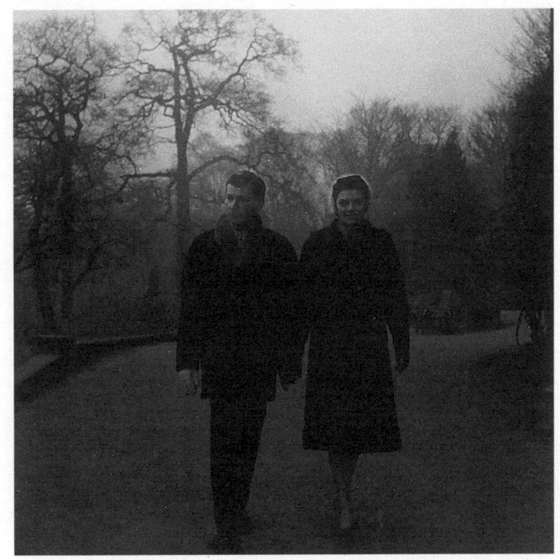

Franz Kempf and Betty, London, 1959

The sensibility of the artist who has access to an inner reservoir of imagery that is incomprehensible, inconceivable or unavailable to the common person, except perhaps in vivid dreams, is a feature that has been under attack in post-modernism, a theory that has viewed the notion of originality as false. For some theorists, post-modern art can be categorised by a lack of spontaneity and expression in its construction, with those elements substituted with pastiche and disruption. Others believe that the object of post-modernism is to challenge the hegemonic structures in culture and discourse and to cast light on their hidden and buried aspects. Amid the competing streams, anti-modernism is common: the lumping together of everything from a previous era as clichéd and irrelevant.

In doing so, just as the modernists tended to reject stagnating methods of traditional art, post-modernism denies the legitimacy of hard-won visual experience, and the range, variety, and subtleties of modernism. The artist of modernist disposition attempts to weld personal conceptions, visions and dreams

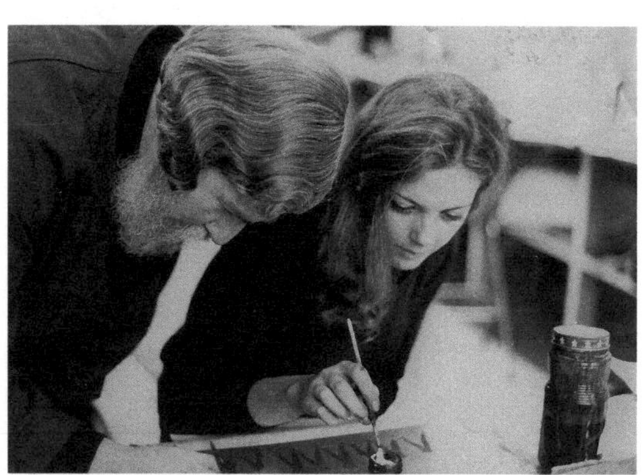

Franz Kempf and student Sally Whisson, first year of printmaking diploma course, South Australian School of Art, 1971

to reality, through practical experience and acquired technical skill. The modernist artist has knowledge of the third, innermost circle, and has had to learn the means by which to realise and communicate the core of his or her art. In contrast, post-modern art seems disinterested in such intense personal experience, preferring instead to lurk on the surface, patching together elements or ironically immersing itself in the dazzle and glamour of its more accessible outer stratum.

And yet, Franz Kempf's work has elements that do connect with post-modern thinking: a more mature method which does not reject but learns from the past. His work has a range and depth that is unusual within modernism, particularly of the later period, as if he has been aware of the potential stereotyping of his work. This accounts for the stylistic range and diverse themes, sometimes overtly political, of his *oeuvre*. He has investigated the worlds of abstraction and figuration, and combined them both. He has shied away from the now familiar structures of rhetorical opposition that were enshrined within the modernist period: the 'apolitical virtue' that despised Realism; and the political virtue that detested Abstraction as 'bourgeois idealism and mystification'. The two positions that argued against each other interminably and refused to concede intellectual ground.[7]

Despite his activism in advancing the art of printmaking, his long and productive teaching career, and his reputation as an artist of considerable aesthetic and conceptual ability, in spirit Franz Kempf resides with a group that tends to live in the shadows of the mythical 'giants'.[8] Artists of essentially European temperaments like Kevin Connor, Gareth Sansom and Andrew Sibley might be classified as standing alongside others of European migrant backgrounds. As such, Franz Kempf represents the multicultural aspect of Australian art, which is becoming more meaningful, rather than the jingoistic, nationalistic impulse that dominated well beyond the first half of the last century. There is good reason for the careers of 'European-Australian' artists to be re-examined, as their eclecticism may well offer intellectual substance and fertile conceptual ground. Certainly such illumination would promote a less elitist view, and one of a much healthier and more vigorous stream of modernism in Australia in the post-war years than has so far been acknowledged.

Franz Kempf's printmaking has been widely acclaimed as groundbreaking and fundamentally significant in the development of the medium in this country. However, the medium of the print itself is somewhat overlooked now, partly because of the light-sensitivity of paper, but also because of the ascendancy of photography and its digitalisation in contemporary art, and the multi-skilling and less specialised approach of artists these days. Since the demise of Tynte Gallery in Adelaide in the late 1980s, the apogee of the medium locally, the print's prominence has declined in South Australia. Not since *Selections of a Century*, a travelling exhibition of prints shown at the Education Centre in Adelaide in 1981, has the Art Gallery of South Australia presented any kind of print survey.[9] Nevertheless, art prints in Australia have been collected in plenitude by the major museums, and Franz Kempf is well-represented among them. It is surprising, therefore, not to find him among the list of artists in the catalogue produced by the Art Gallery of New South Wales in 1998.[10] Nevertheless, he is well represented in Sasha Grishin's recent books on Australian printmaking, and in international publications.

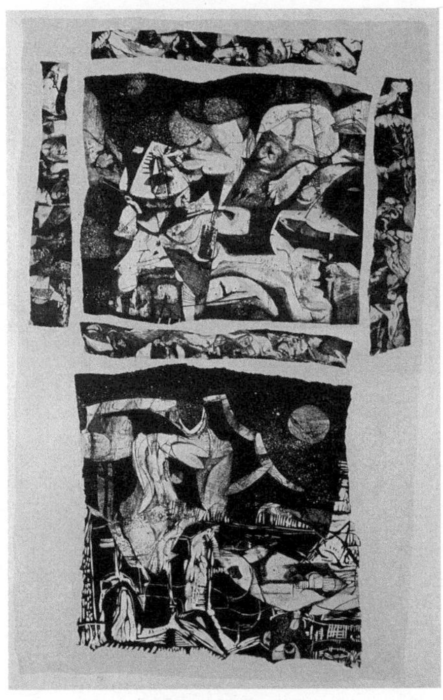

Space Probe, 1973

Grishin comments that Kempf's 'lyricism can give way to unbridled aggression',[11] but seldom, if ever, does aggression rule. It simply does not fit with the artist's temperament or artistic philosophy, wherein sharp intelligence, sensitivity to his materials, and an involved conversation with art and its history are conducive to successful outcomes. One can glean this in the artist's committed choice of forms. They are never reduced to rigid geometry, except in the use of the Star of David, and seldom contain straight lines, unless obliquely referring to a broken horizon in a landscape, or rectangular windows, tables or doors in still life or interior compositions. Generally, his visual language is built on deeply symbolic, more complex geometry, his shapes derived from the figure and nature and, when less abstract, an expressive, free line and layering of sensual texture and delicate colour. As Franz Kempf explains, 'When one creates a private language it is one's way of describing the world, to remain sane, to find one's way.'[12]

It is clear from his notes and the titles of his work that Franz Kempf is inspired by artists in other fields, especially music and literature. Elements from such diverse sources as traditional Talmudic to contemporary Yiddish texts, Percy Bysshe Shelley, Emily Dickinson, D.H. Lawrence, and Patrick White pervade his imagery. He can work more or less conventionally or metaphorically, according to his mood and conception, as seen in the numerous paintings and prints, such as the series titled *Finestra* (1977) and *Windows* (1978), that refer to the interior, architecturally and spiritually.

The *Coorong* series of the early 1980s was the catalyst that brought the artist back from the extremes of abstraction, still evident in 1970s' work such as *Space Probe* (1973) and the series *Reflections on Bashevis Singer* (1979), to representing the landscape.[13] These works refer to early watercolours of East Anglia in the 1950s and the poetry of the triptych called *Morning Departure* (1974).[14] At times, the delicacy in this series approaches the sublime or numinous. Whether in drypoint etching, lithograph or pen and wash drawings, this theme enabled Kempf to use the white of the page to convey the distinct, wide and vast space of sand and pale sea and sky, sparse vegetation and idiosyncratic light. It broke with his previous style of a denser compilation of tone and texture (and sometimes text), and sent him on a renewed aesthetic journey that celebrated the line and a gentler touch.

Donald Brook commented on Kempf's new style of work in 1989:

In these landscapes and interiors painted in England, in France, in Israel and in Australia, the common theme is an objectified delight expressed – to put it badly – in the luscious painterly terms of Impressionism. But projected into the innocent field, with an increasingly convincing show of objectivity, are the tones or images of malediction borrowed from Expressionism: the lowering sky, the twisted shadow that is more active than the light, the window frame that is a cage, the minatory hulks of concrete left over from the worst of wars.

Poignancy is the most difficult of moods to sustain in art. On the one side sentimentality beckons; on the other side lie the blandishments of that theatrical morbidity by which so much of the Symbolist art of the last [nineteenth] century was debauched. In his maturity and with his eyes wide open Franz Kempf has set out, without flourish, to deny both of these enchanters a new victim.[15]

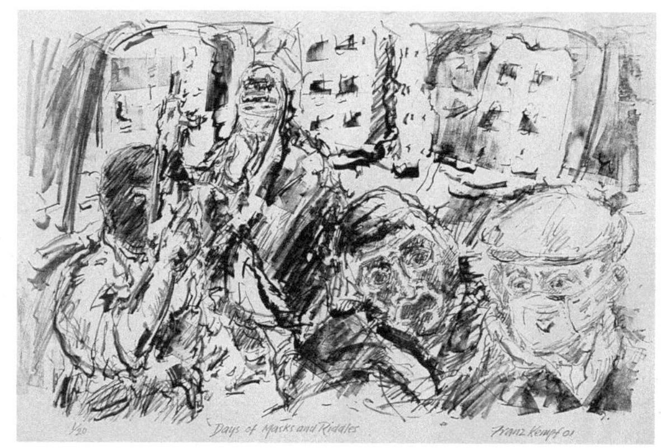

Days of Masks and Riddles, 2001

The gentler and unflourished touch is evident in the most recent series in both watercolour and print, such as the macabre *Days of Masks and Riddles* (2001), with its reference to the war in the Balkans or prophetically to the apocalyptic scenes of 11 September 2001 in New York, and *The Garden* (2001), which revisits an earlier theme of the Gardens of Bomarzi.[16] The artist first encountered this surreal sculptural space in 1956 and it has haunted his imagination since. It is inhabited by 'petrified monsters' and was built in Italy by Duke Vincento Orsini in 1561 seemingly as a monument to his deceased wife.[17] Kempf tends to reconnect with previously abandoned threads and then weave these visual stories onwards, often contemporaneously with work of quite disparate tendencies.

Another recent series reflects on the interior theme once more, focusing also on the solitary voyage of the artist, depicting views of his own back garden from his studio window, in front of which he has placed a row of model ships. The pared-down lithographs in ochre and black titled *Navigating the Past* and *Strange Passage* link the hard-won values of experience with the fanciful hopes of youth. Franz Kempf observes:

Though I have this desire to withdraw to my spiritual nirvana in the studio, or garden surrounding it, it is not possible, despite disillusion with the values of politics, religion and finance close to my door. Just as Yaakov's struggle with the angel changes his name to Israel, so my struggle changes perceptions – experience is not possible without involvement. Whether this produces Jewish art or not I leave to those who bust themselves with computers or index categories – my concern is to produce works that convey some information about known objects, what I dream of, remember or ardently desire. By producing these images I am able to chart a course for myself through the world, less than ideal and at times very intangible.[18]

Over time, fashions in art change, but substance and intelligence remain true and discernible, and continue to engage the art lover. With a grander, more lasting interpretation of the value of art, Franz Kempf maintains his vision and delivers with consistency and increasing ease the qualities that endure in art. His is not the art of a hopeful youngster, aimed desperately at the stars, but rather, it is stardust itself.

***Adam Dutkiewicz** completed a degree in Communication Studies at the South Australian College of Art and Education and Honours at the University of South Australia. He has been an art critic for the Adelaide* Advertiser, *and written regularly for* Business Review Weekly *and* Art Monthly Australia Online. *He has recently been awarded a PhD in Art History and Theory.*

1 My father, Wladyslaw, won it in its inaugural year.

2 Students could elect to major in printmaking and related subjects, book production and photography, over three years.

3 See George Berger, *Franz Kempf*, Brolga Books, 1969; N. Weston, *Franz Kempf: graphic works 1962–1984*, Wakefield Press, 1984; R. Brooks, *Franz Kempf*, Craftsman House, 1991

4 Handwritten notes to the author, January 2002

5 Franz Kempf acknowledges the influences of Oskar Kokoshka, as he attended his school in Salzburg, along with Alfred Kubin and Emil Nolde, as well as the American abstract expressionists. He met Afro and was introduced to the work of Santomaso.

6 L. Goldberg, paraphrased by F. Kempf in referring to his *Jerusalem* tapestry, typed notes, c. 1987. Comments by conductor Henry Krips on such relationships in the artist's work are also illuminating. See H. Krips in N. Weston, op. cit., opposite chronology, np.

7 Charles Harrison and Paul Wood (eds), 'Introduction: Ideas of the Postmodern', *Art in Theory, 1900–1990: An Anthology of Changing Ideas*, Blackwell, 1992, p 988.

8 Indeed, Bernard Smith, in his watershed book *Australian Painting* records him as an Austrian émigré artist. See B. Smith, 'The Art Scene', *Australian Painting 1788–1970*, 2nd edition, Oxford University Press, 1971, pp 336–37.

9 This situation is being admirably addressed by Adele Boag in her Main Street Editions Gallery at Hahndorf, South Australia.

10 Kempf is represented in their collection.

11 Sasha Grishin, 'The Golden Age of Printmaking in Australia', Contemporary Australian Printmaking: an interpretative history, Craftsman House, 1994, p 104

12 Handwritten notes to author, *ibid.*

13 Indeed, as Weston notes, Kempf's work 'evinces the qualities of a character from the world of Bashevis Singer, someone standing between the past and the present, unable to embrace either wholeheartedly . . .' N. Weston, 'Introduction', Franz Kempf, *op. cit.*, p 7.

14 Indeed, a bridging work in pastel, dated from 1981, was titled East Anglia.

15 D. Brook, typed notes, 1989

16 A series of aquatint etchings on this theme was produced in 1963.

17 F. Kempf, typed notes, 2000

18 Typed notes to the author, January 2002

IMITATIONS OF INFINITUDE

ROBERT SMITH

Report of fashion in proud Italy,
Whose manners still our tardy, apish nation
Limps after in base imitation . . .

Thus William Shakespeare in *Richard II* comments on the persistent phenomenon of cultural dependence. The observation is significant for our alienated and eclectic age – without needing the imposition of spurious 'relevance', so typical of our times. The work of Franz Kempf embodies comparably broad significance. Intrinsic motivations give his art a depth and intensity beyond fashionable externals.

Art of all times and societies is capable of bridging gulfs of cultural difference. The best art is grounded in its community's most fundamental ethical values, and thereby discernible across cultures despite disparities of social conditioning. This is no mere issue of simplistic 'communication' – that passing fad of specious academic populism. Profound and enduring art does not exhaust itself instantaneously in minimalist 'communication' but repays renewed perusal, constantly yielding fresh insights into the human condition. Nor is this a matter of reading our own concerns into the products of other cultures, but of coming to grips with their innate significance. Otherwise we debase the art of others into symbols of our own discontent, or – perhaps worse – into exotic décor for our culture of affluent decadence.

All this is highly relevant when considering Franz Kempf's art, particularly since it is embedded in two distinct cultures. An Australian, aware of our transformation of the European heritage in this part of the world, he is also deeply involved with Jewish tradition. This duality creates a sense of commitment, not just to each of those cultures but to a broader view emphasising the tenacity and worth of human life. He looks on existence as a chain with many links, and his art moves back and forth through time and space, establishing a feeling for the potentially infinite.

What endows this cosmic quality with validity and conviction is its constant perceptive reference to place and time-specific motifs as diverse as ancient Jerusalem, wind-swept South Australian dunes, and space exploration. It encompasses many facets of life: cultural, historical, the erotic, environmental, technological, artistic heritage and its permutations, the joys of self-realisation in artistic technique, and the media which impinge on all these areas of experience.

There are sequences of Kempf prints which develop various aspects of a theme. They may lay bare the horrendous bureaucratic efficiency with which the Holocaust documented its dehumanised iniquities – as in *Memorial I, II* and *III*, which are deeply moving by their very understatement. Or, like the *Coorong* series, celebrate life through lyrical meditation on the redeeming power of nature. These variations on a theme within a group of prints reinforce and illuminate one another in subtle yet

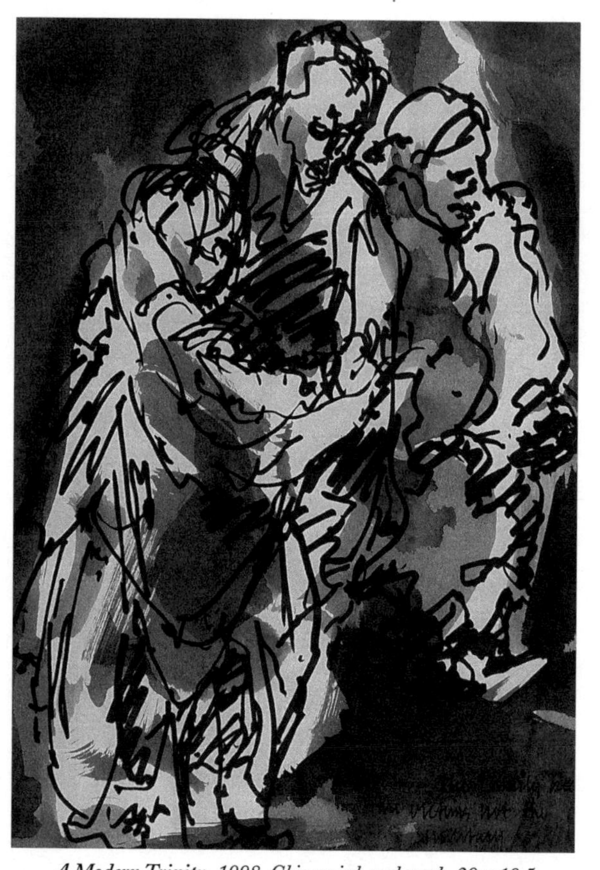

A Modern Trinity, 1998, Chinese ink and wash, 29 x 19.5

cogent ways. Sometimes the variations are compositionally marginal to a central motif – structurally and conceptually resembling calligraphic rubrics surrounding a scriptural text. The lithograph *With Signs and With Wonders* exemplifies this thematic relation between meaning and form, between the part and the whole.

The deliberately symbolic shaping of form is a constant throughout the works, which cannot properly be apprehended without an appreciation of its pervasive energising presence. Symbolic form operates on a subtle yet meaningful metaphorical level, which is figurative in the deepest sense of intrinsic significance, not superficial naturalism on the one hand nor empty formalism on the other. It is not fortuitous that many of the prints are named 'figurations'. This is figuration as a poet or composer might use the term, creating images which reverberate in the awareness rather than solely recording outward appearances.

The same is true of technique. Franz Kempf is an accomplished technician, deploying a range of media, always to illuminate his themes, often combining the timelessness of biblical subjects with the frenzied rate of technological change in this apocalyptic age. In a work such as *Space Probe* the fragments of ancient shards parallel the detritus of space-age exploration in a telling parable for our times.

The prints have a great sense of pictorial integration. Everything works simultaneously on numerous planes. Even the areas of paper showing white are not just negative shapes, but positive design elements contributing to the overall creative effect.

These are pictures to be contemplated, interrogated and deeply pondered. They are – even the tiniest of them – profound distillations of thought and feeling.

***Robert Smith**, art historian, actor, playwright, photographer, critic, and curator, was foundation editor of* Westerly *and the* Australian Journal of Art. *He has helped direct major art museums and founded art studies at Flinders University and its art museum. His photographs have been exhibited throughout Australia.*

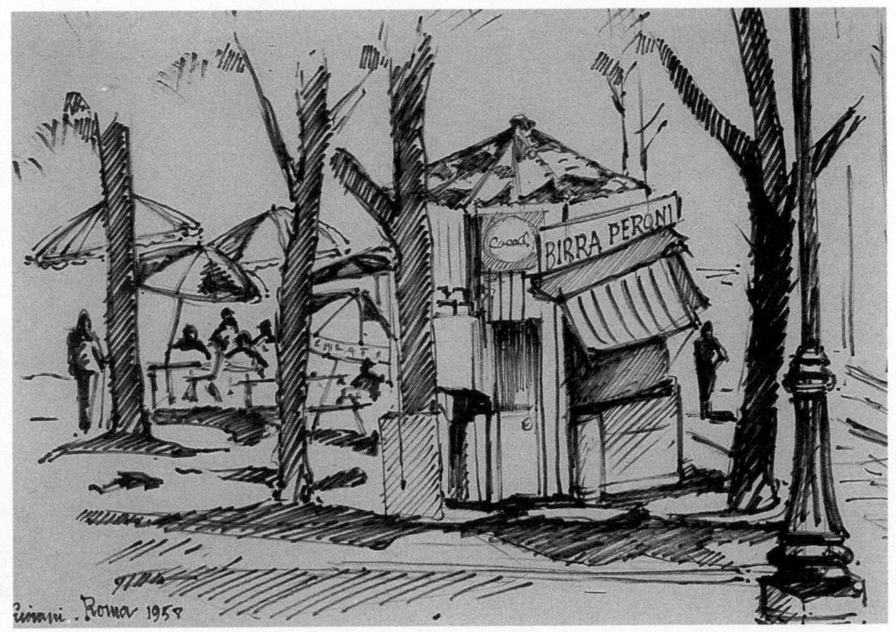

Birra Peroni, 1958, bistre drawing, 17 x 24

FRANZ

I live in a world that is both entrancing and disturbing. Feeling a modicum of social responsibility, I attempt to convey information about the human condition. At times this may be tranquil, expressive of an inner harmony, and often it will be expressive of disquiet, reflecting disillusion with the human condition and its abject state. The demands made by these voices is constant throughout my work.

KEMPF on Paper 1955 – 2002

We must respect the anguished human voice for we all live on this darkling planet threatened by ever growing madness.

By producing images I am able to chart a course for myself through this less than ideal and very intangible world. In such a world one becomes a sceptic or a heretic.

Franz Kempf, 2002

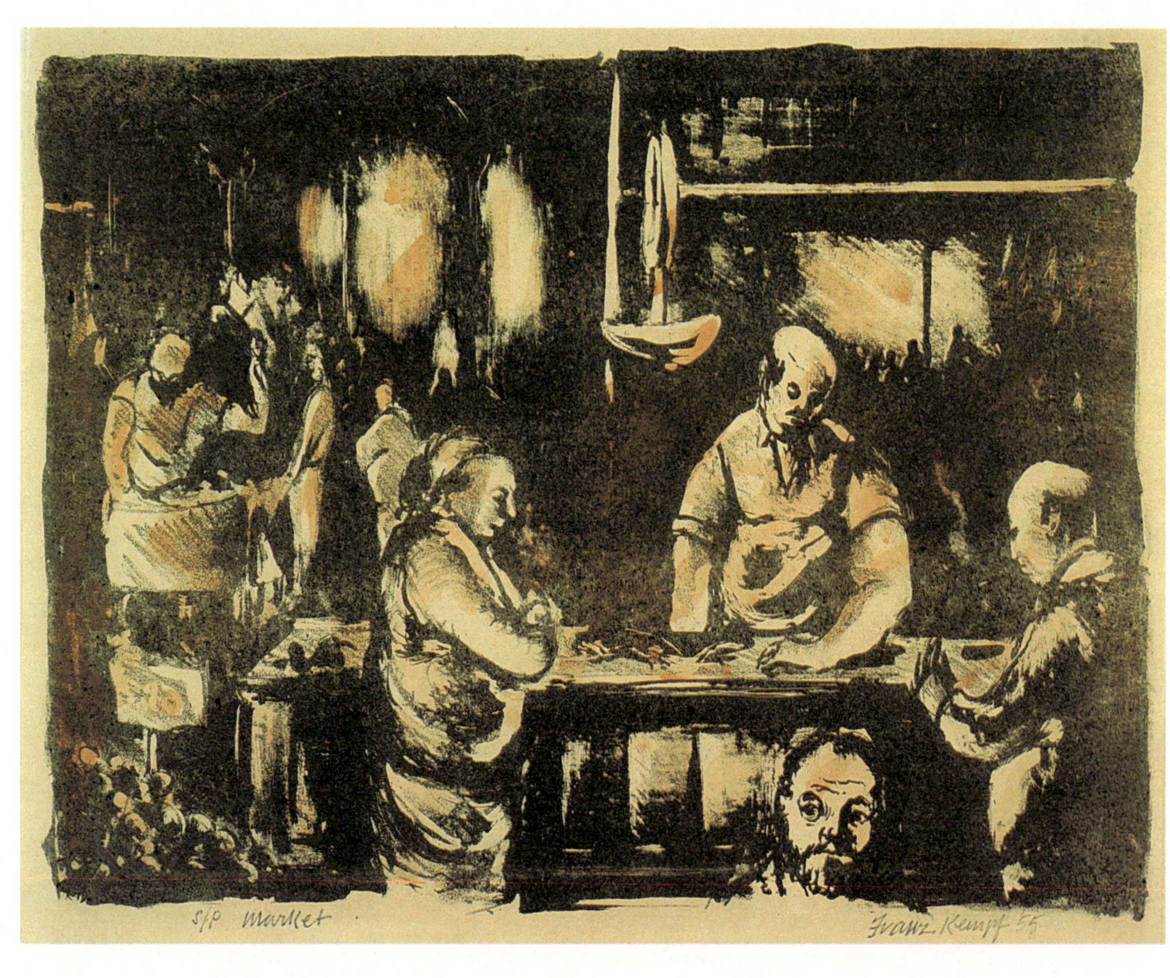

Market – State Proof, 1955, lithograph – two colours, 21 x 27

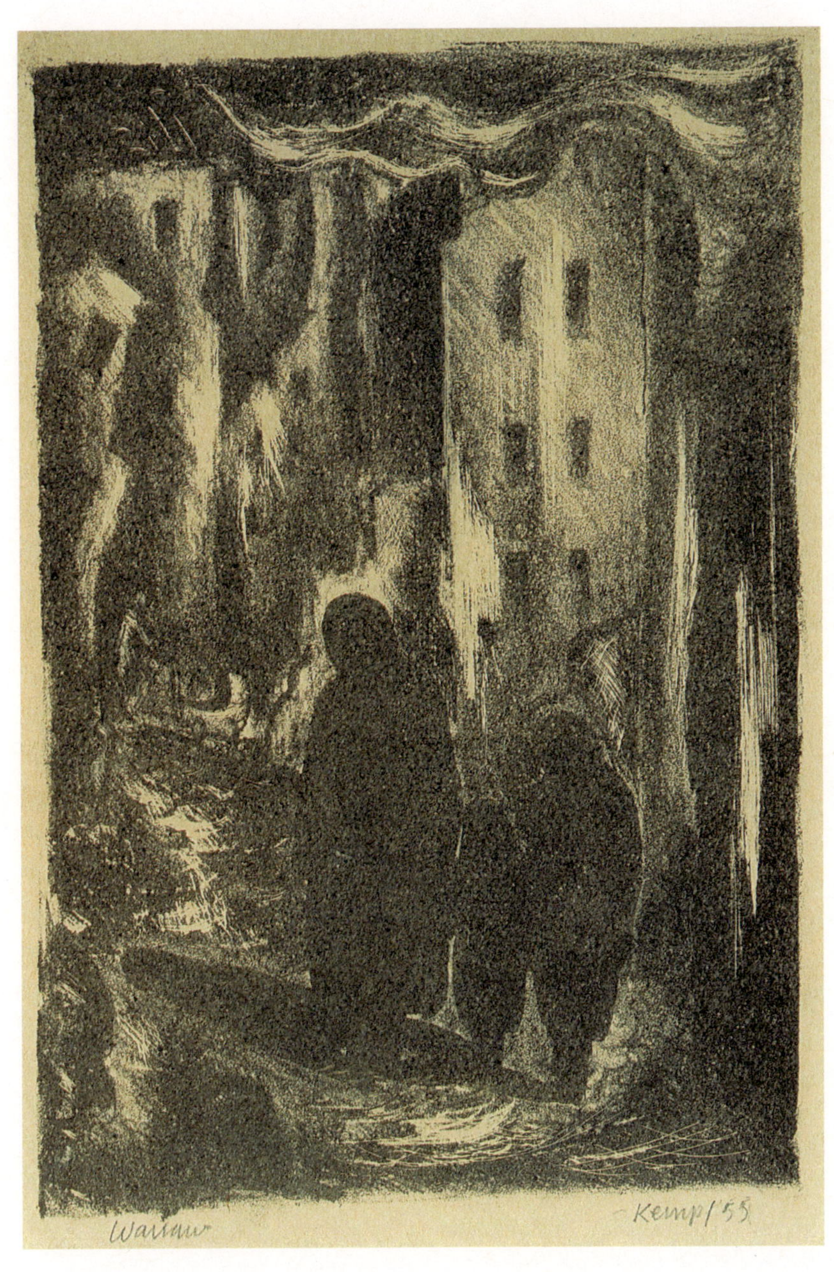

Ghetto Warsaw, 1955, lithograph – black, 22 x 14

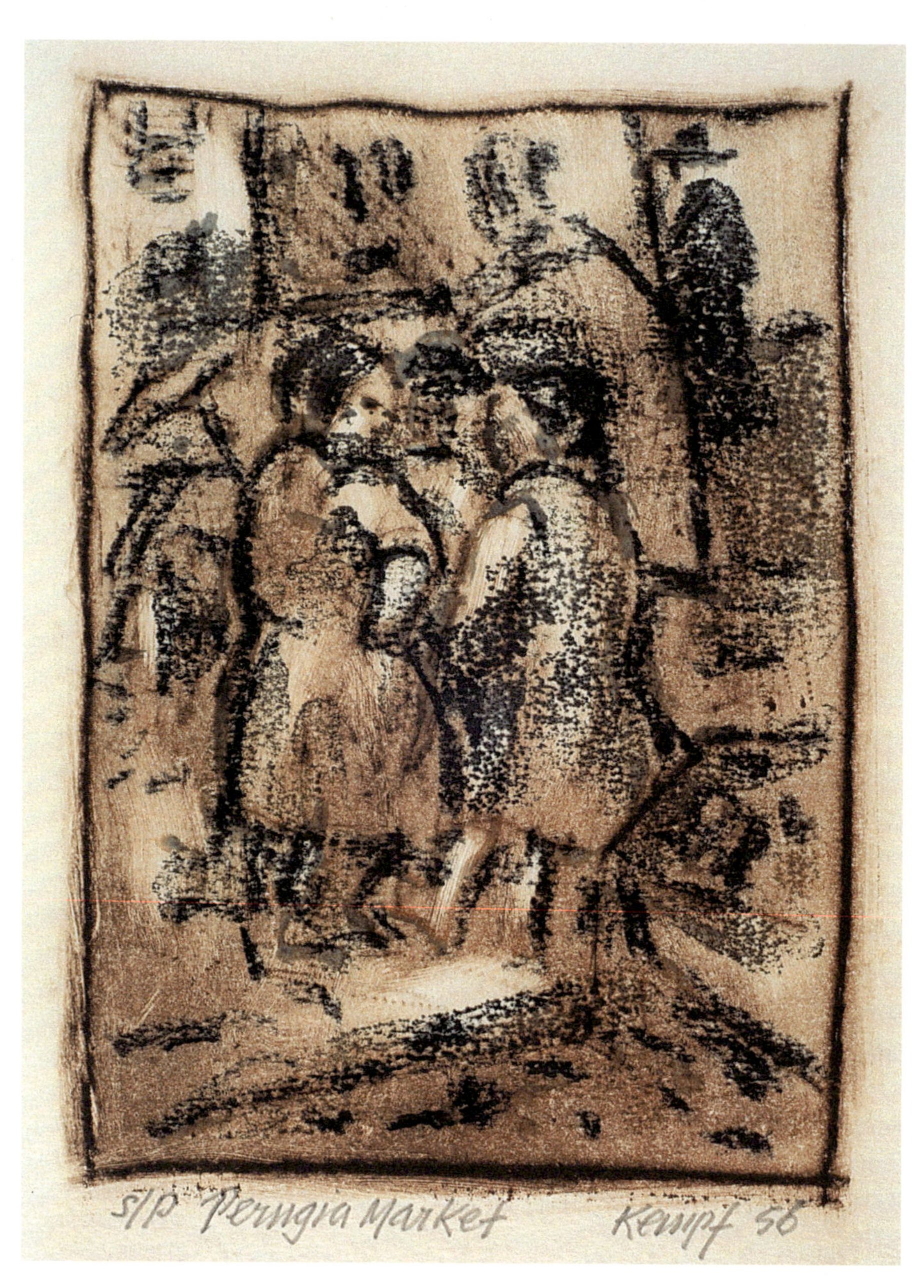

Perugia Street Market, 1956, S/P drypoint black and sepia, 17 x 12

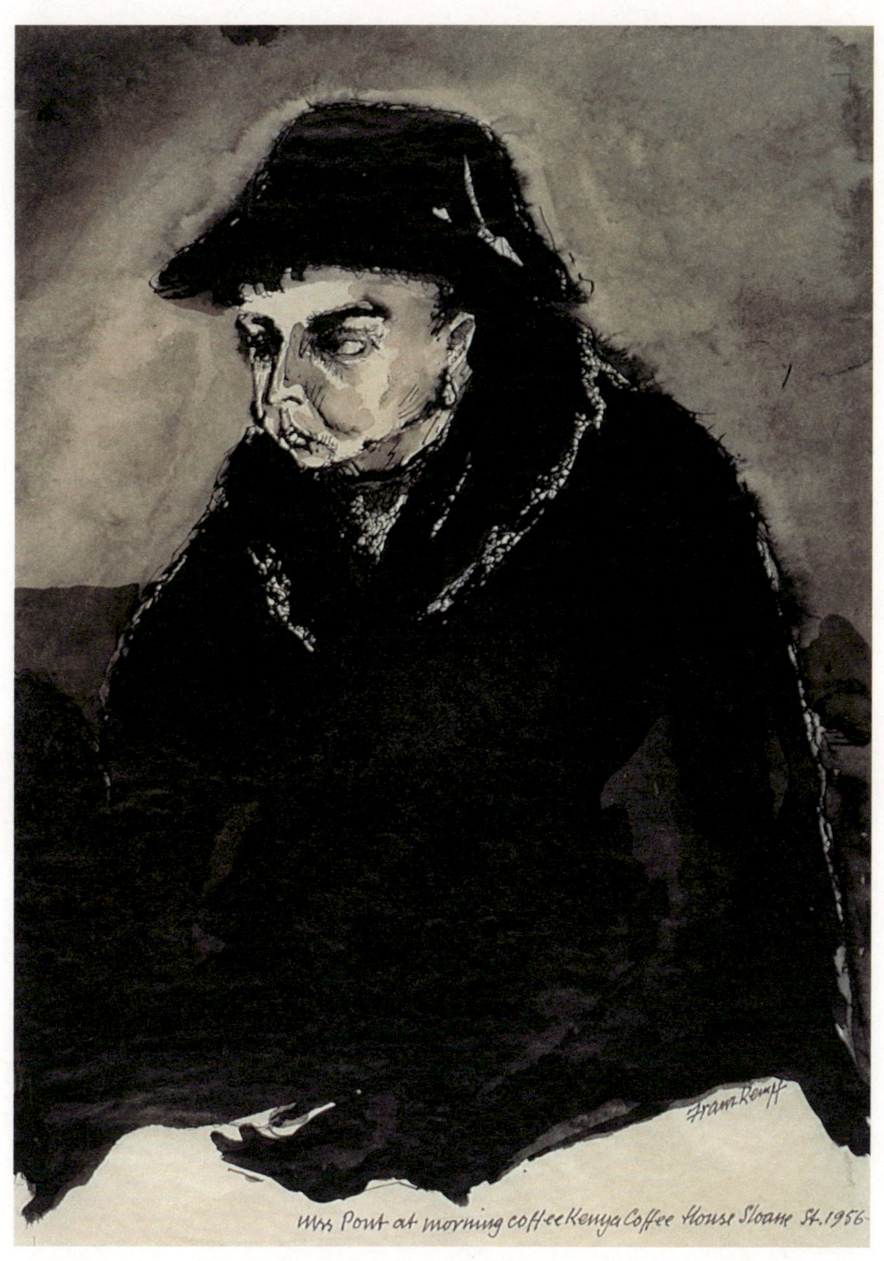

Mrs Pont – Kenya Coffee Lounge, 1956, ink drawing, 31 x 21.5

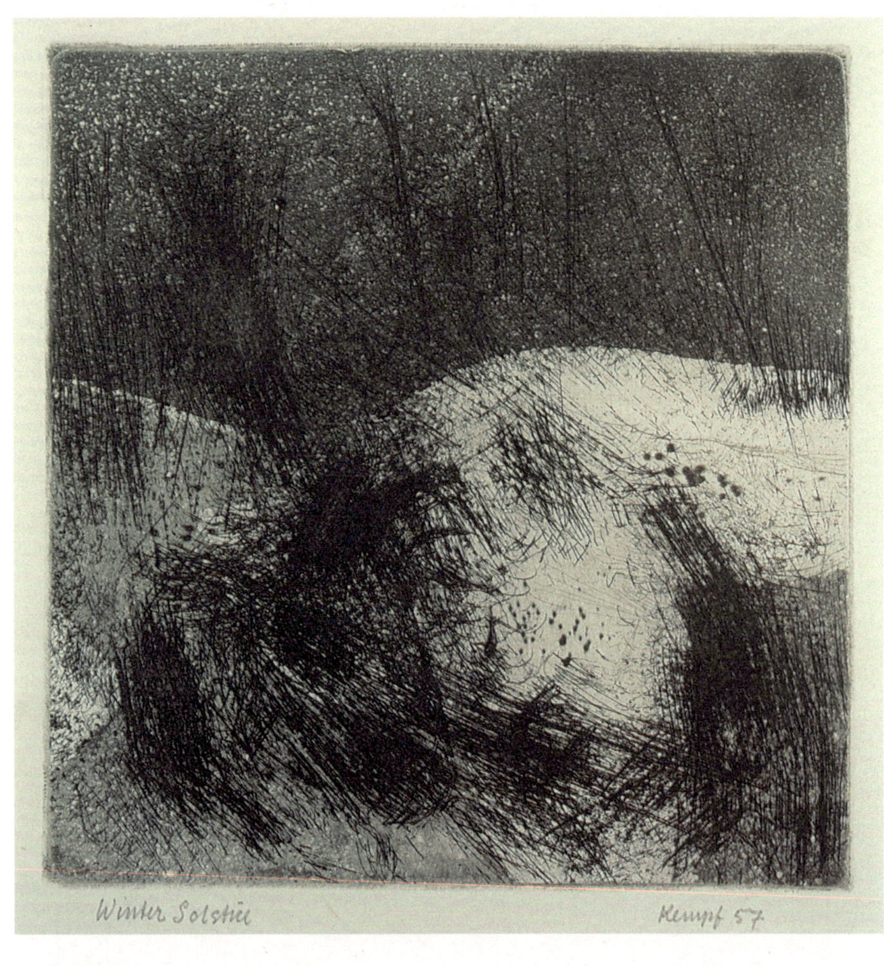

Winter Solstice, 1957, aquatint and etching, 27.5 x 32.5

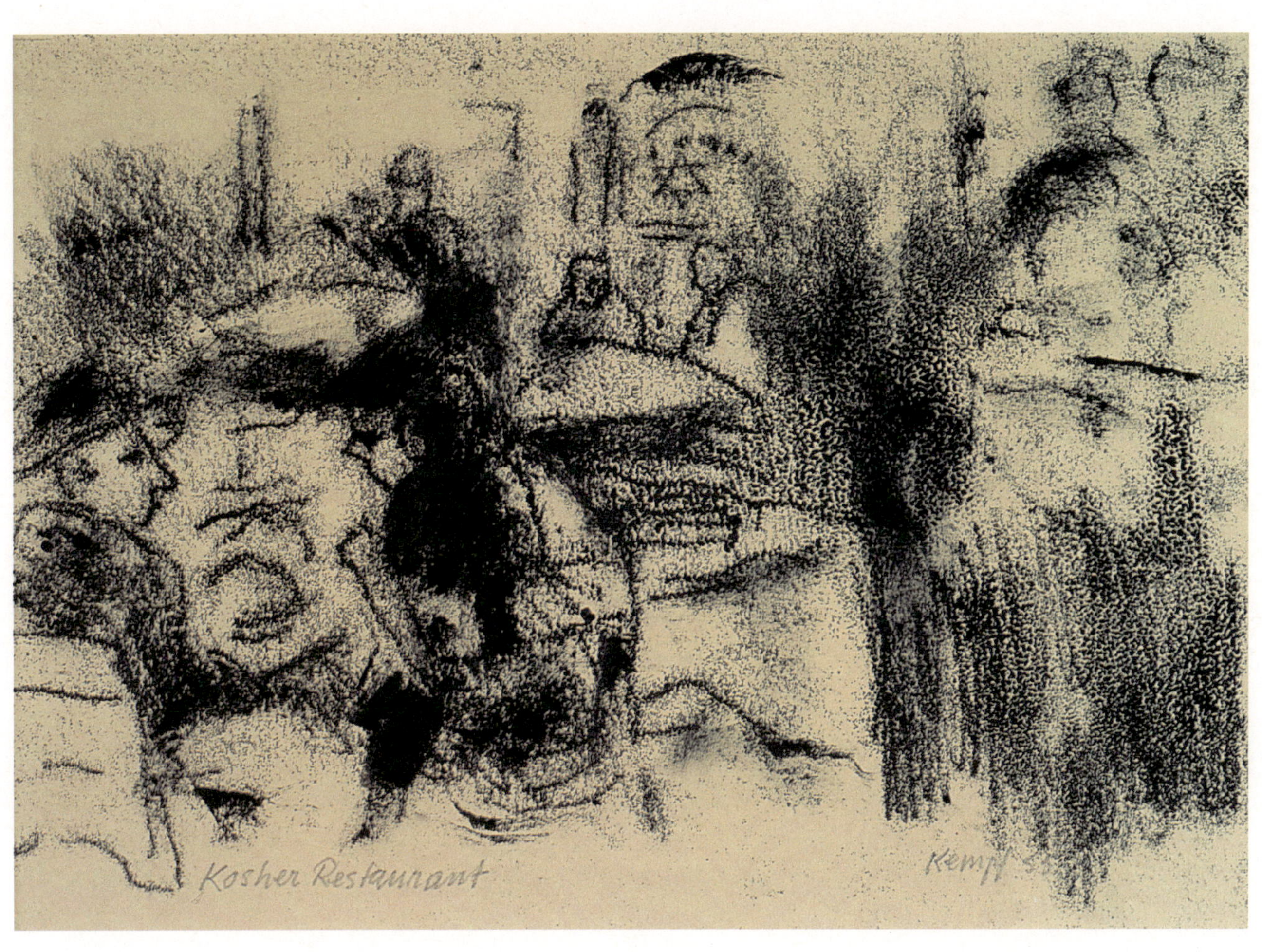

Kosher Restaurant – London, 1958, monotype, 17 x 23.5

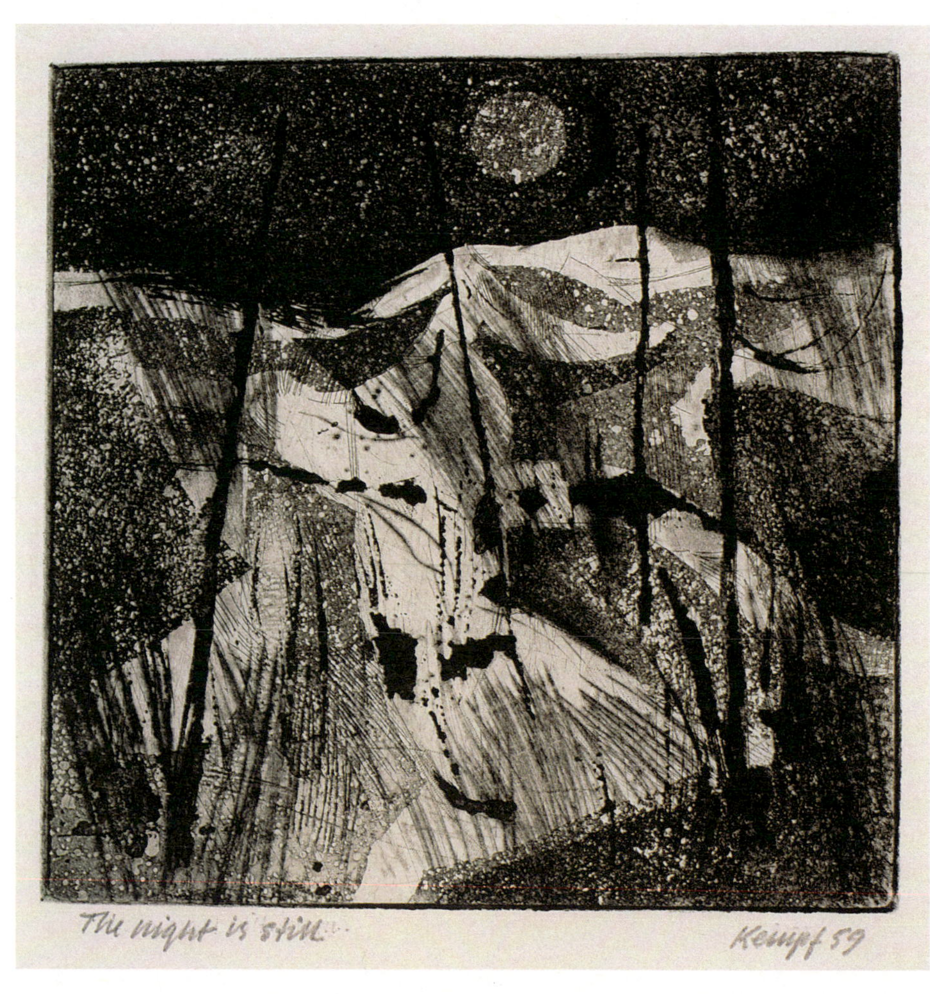

The Night is Still, 1959, aquatint, roulette and drypoint, 16 x 15.5

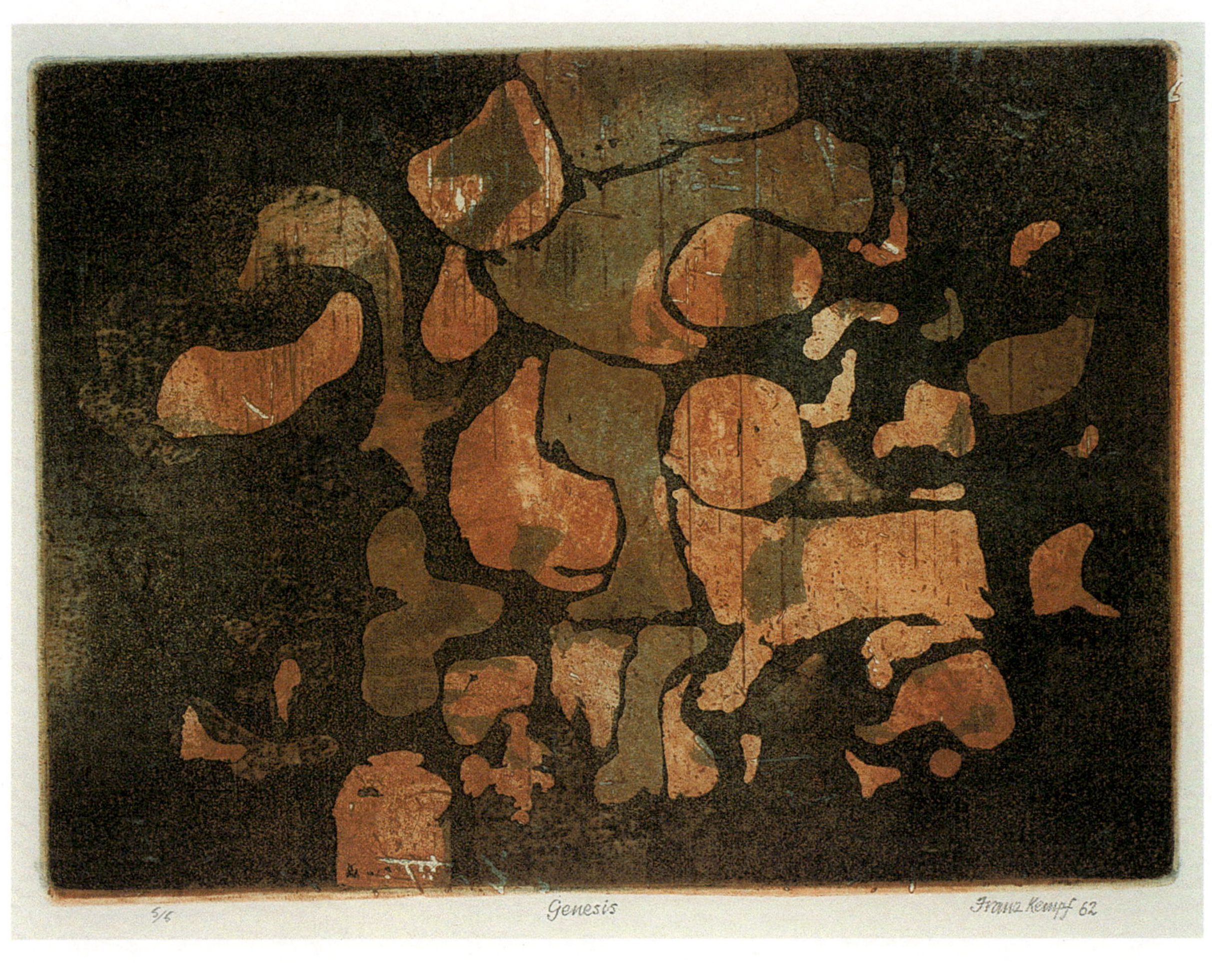

Genesis, 1962, etching and aquatint, 22.5 x 30

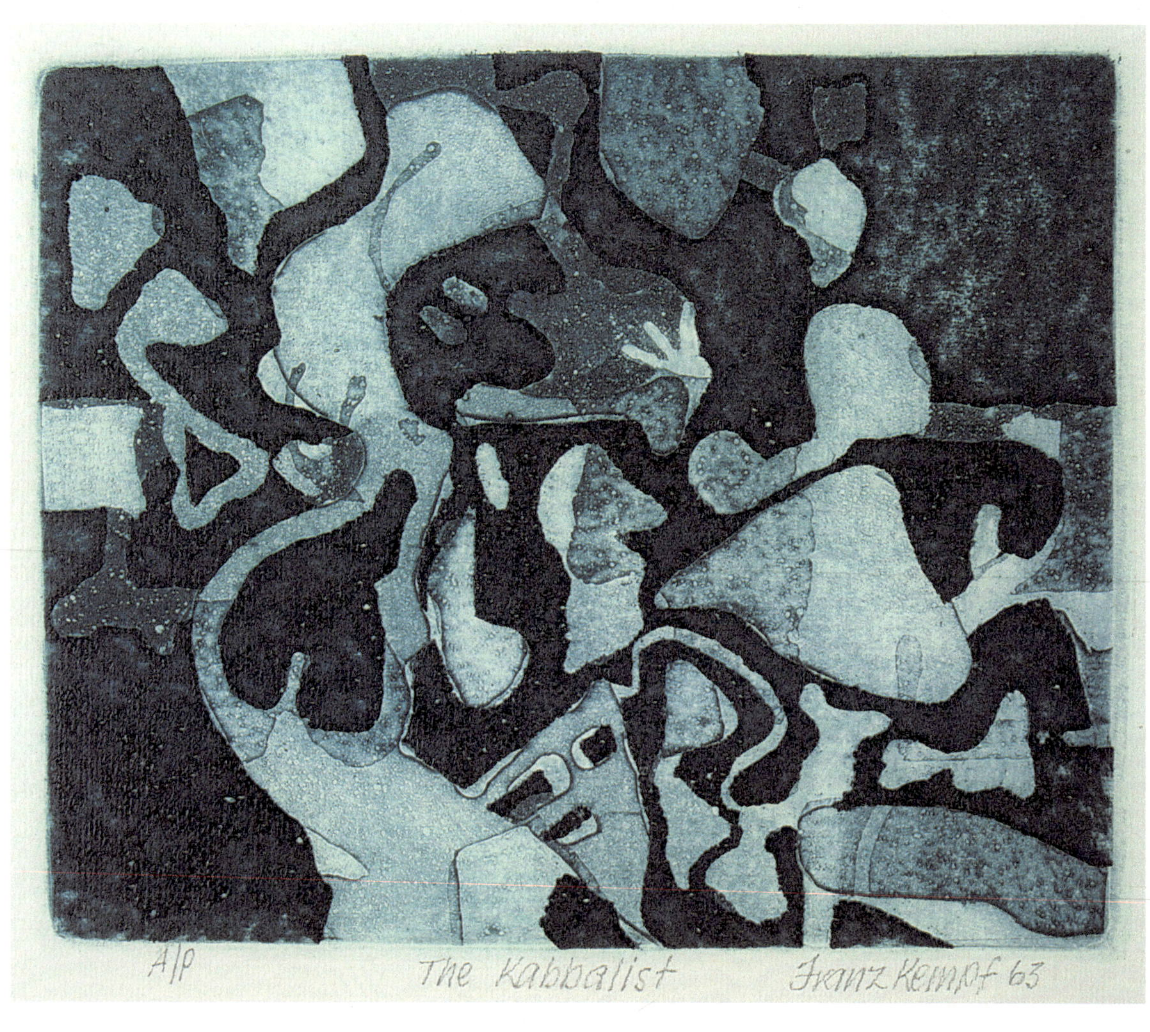

The Kabbalist, 1963, aquatint, 12 x 14

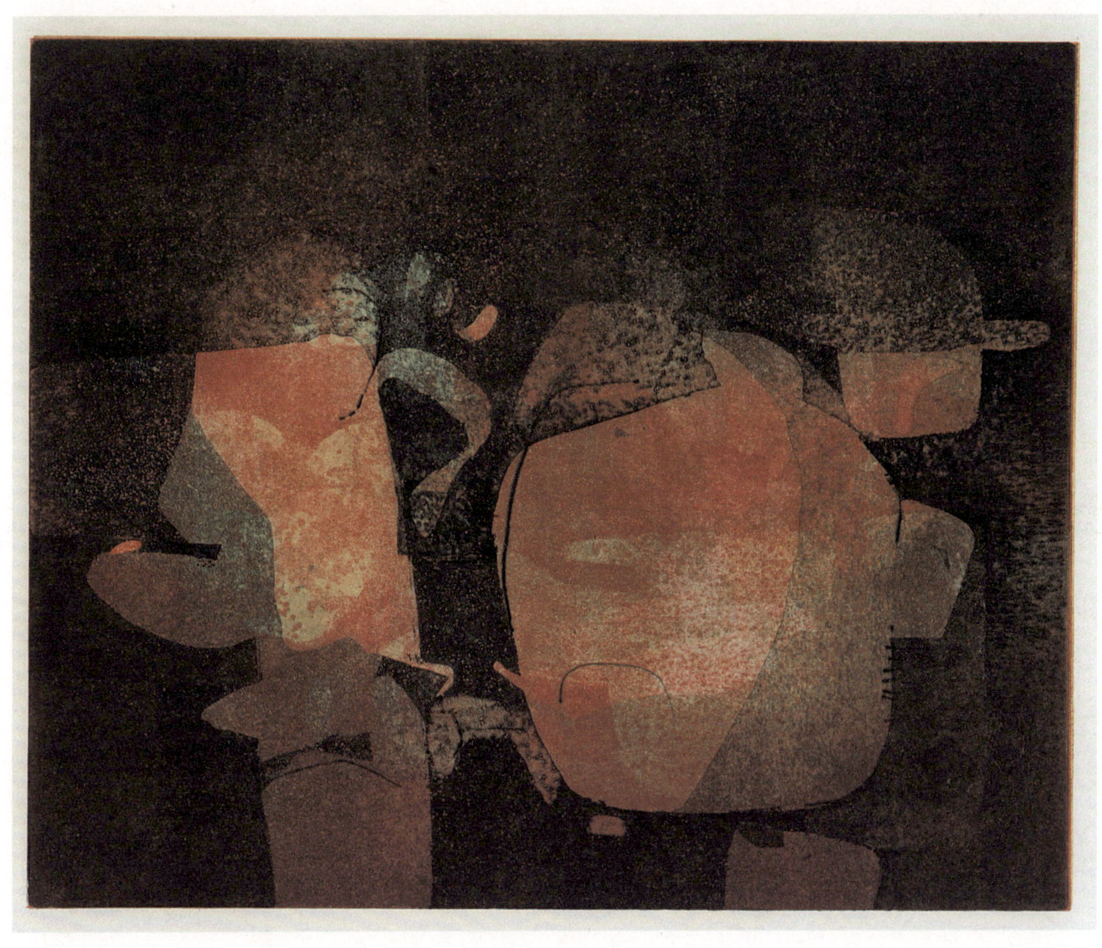

The Garden of Bomarzi II, 1963, aquatint, 27.5 x 32

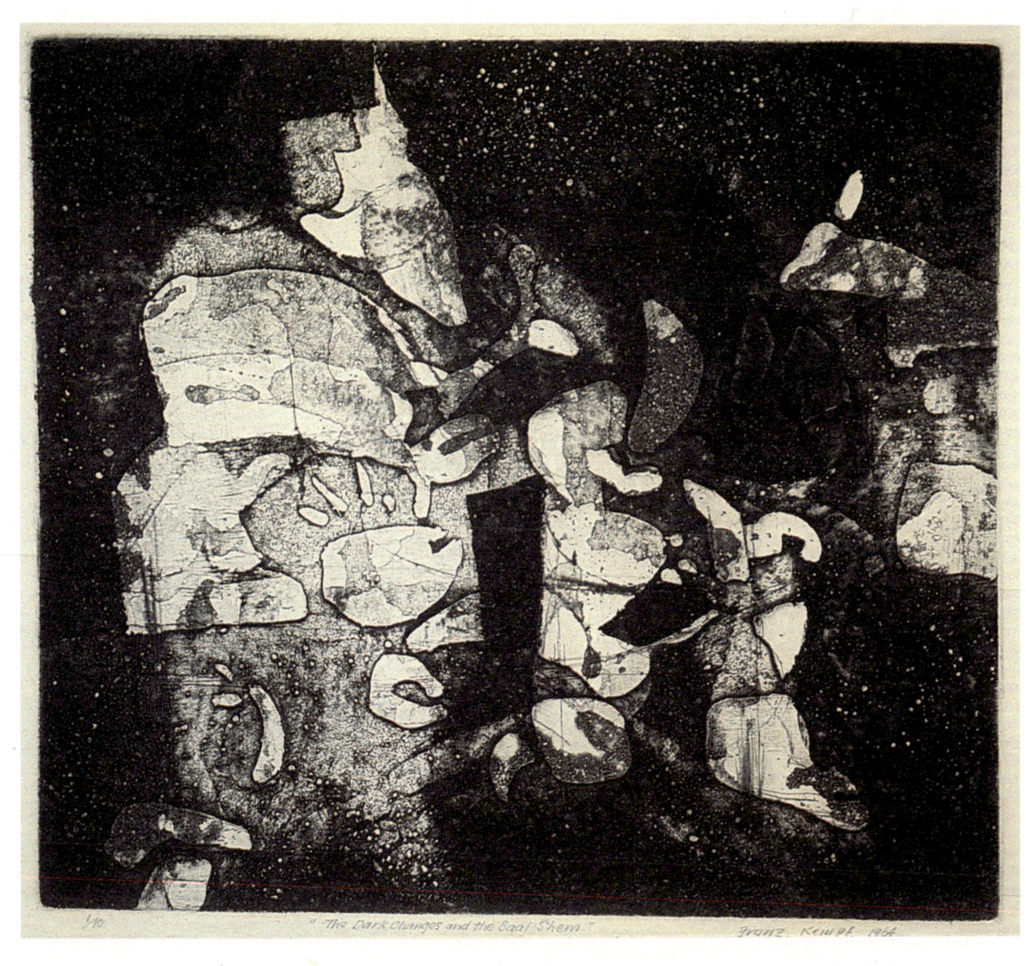

The Dark Changes and The Baal Shem, 1964, etching, aquatint and drypoint, 23 x 25

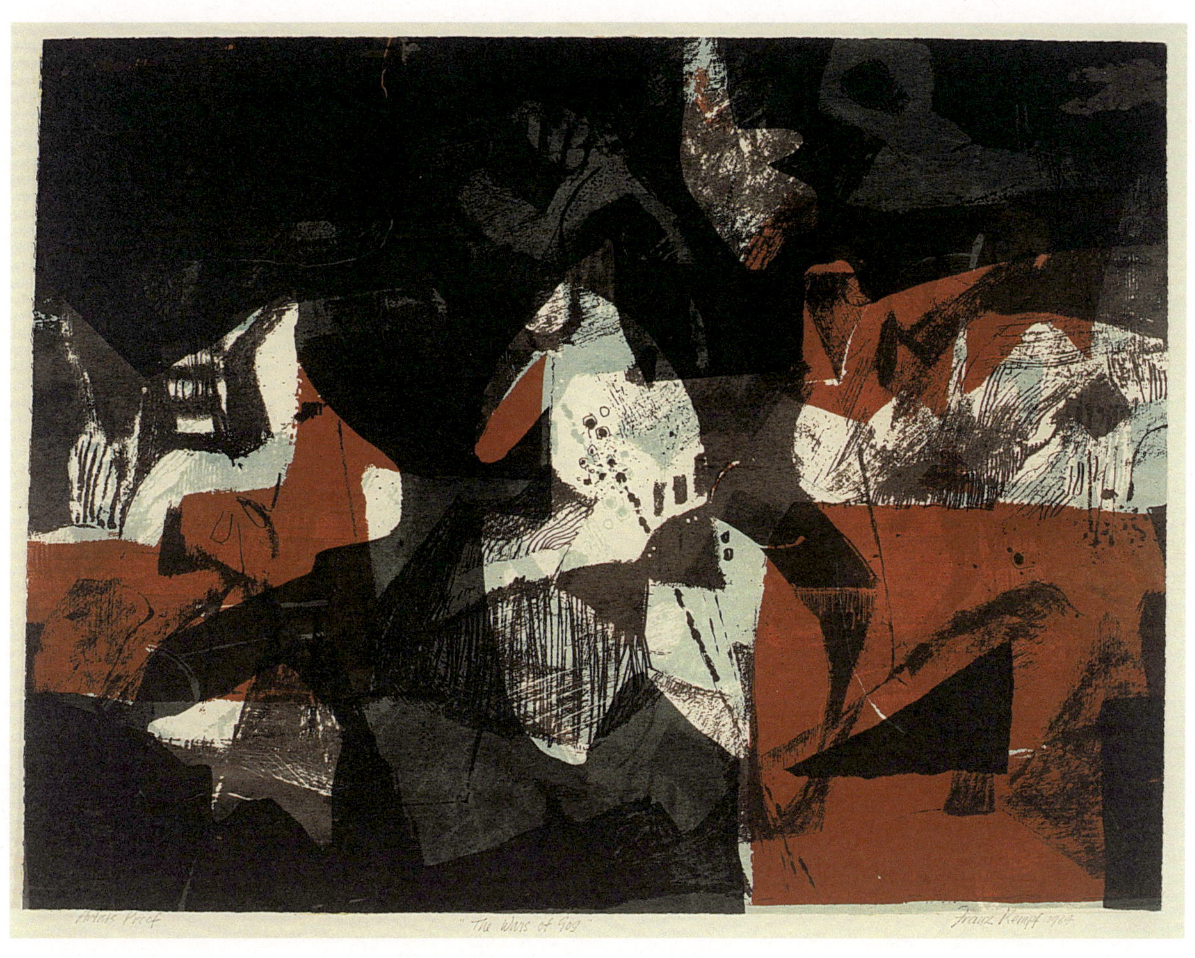

The Wars of GOG II, 1964, screenprint, 47 x 60

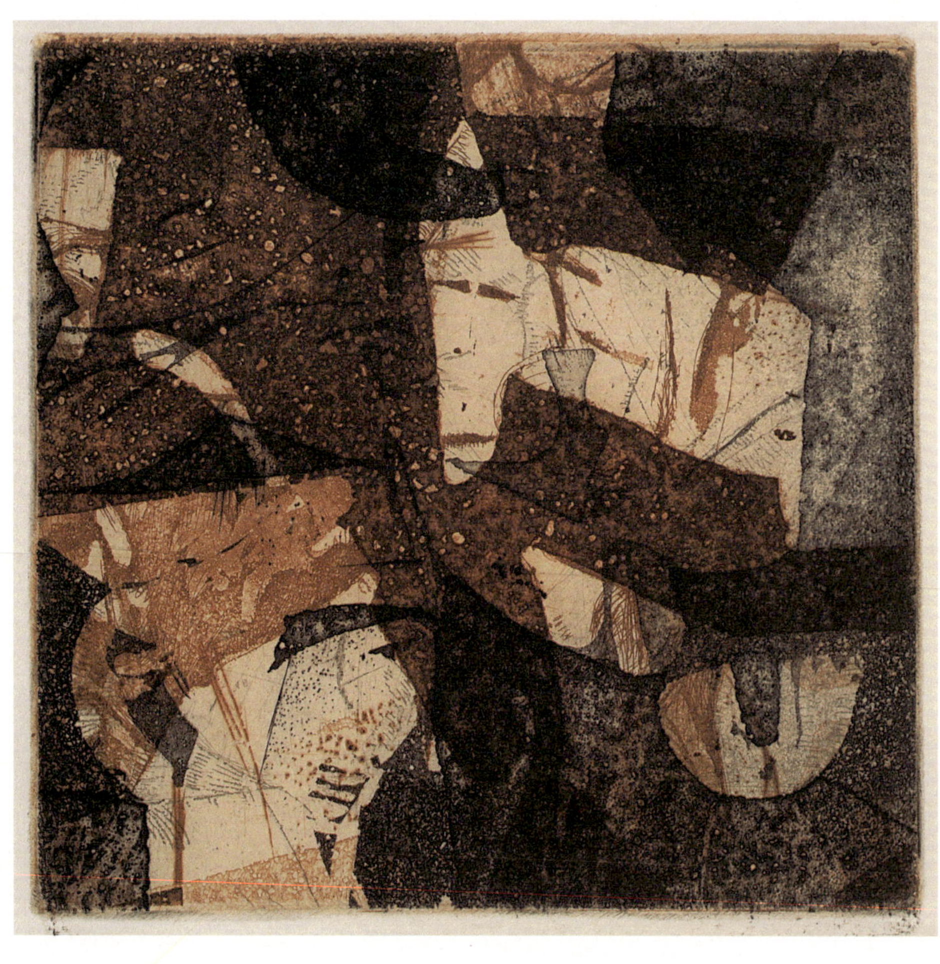

The Prisoner, 1969, etching, aquatint and drypoint, 14 x 14

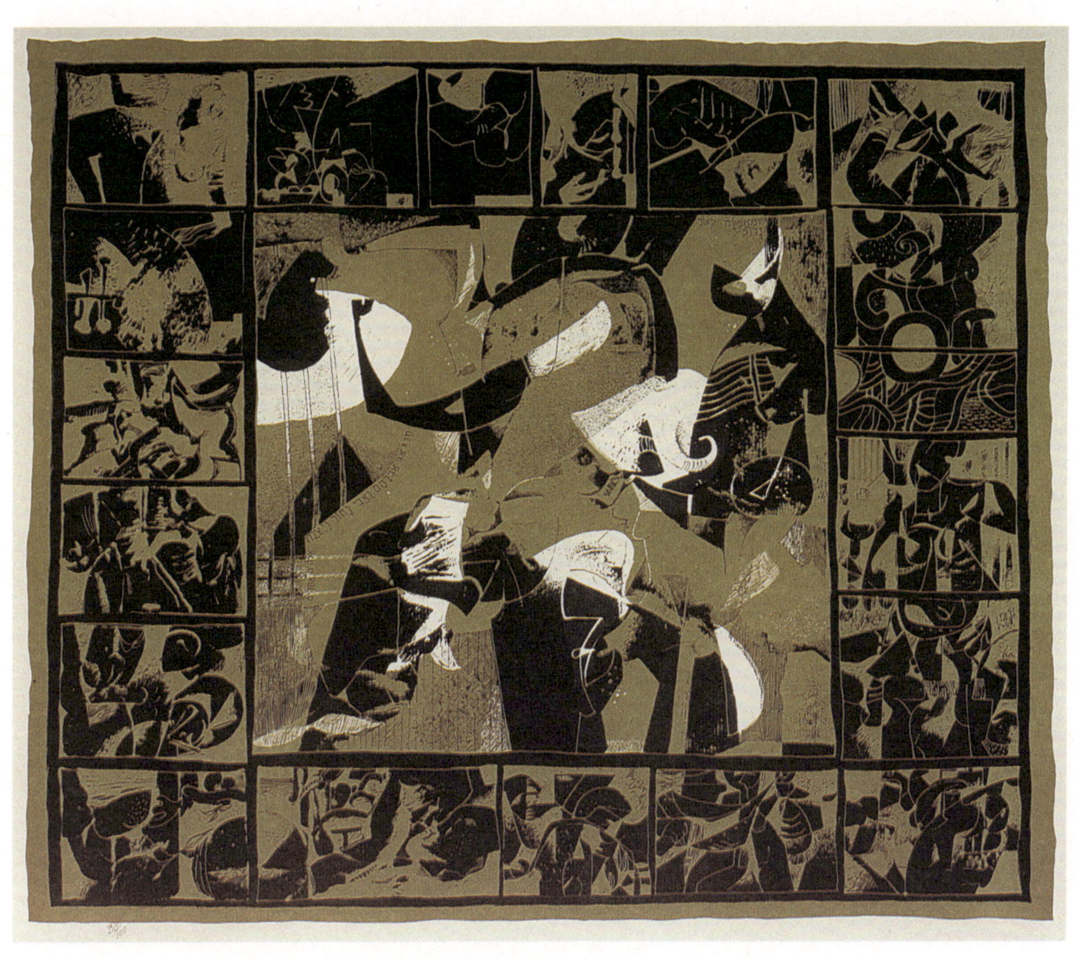

With Signs and With Wonders, 1971, lithograph, 42 x 49

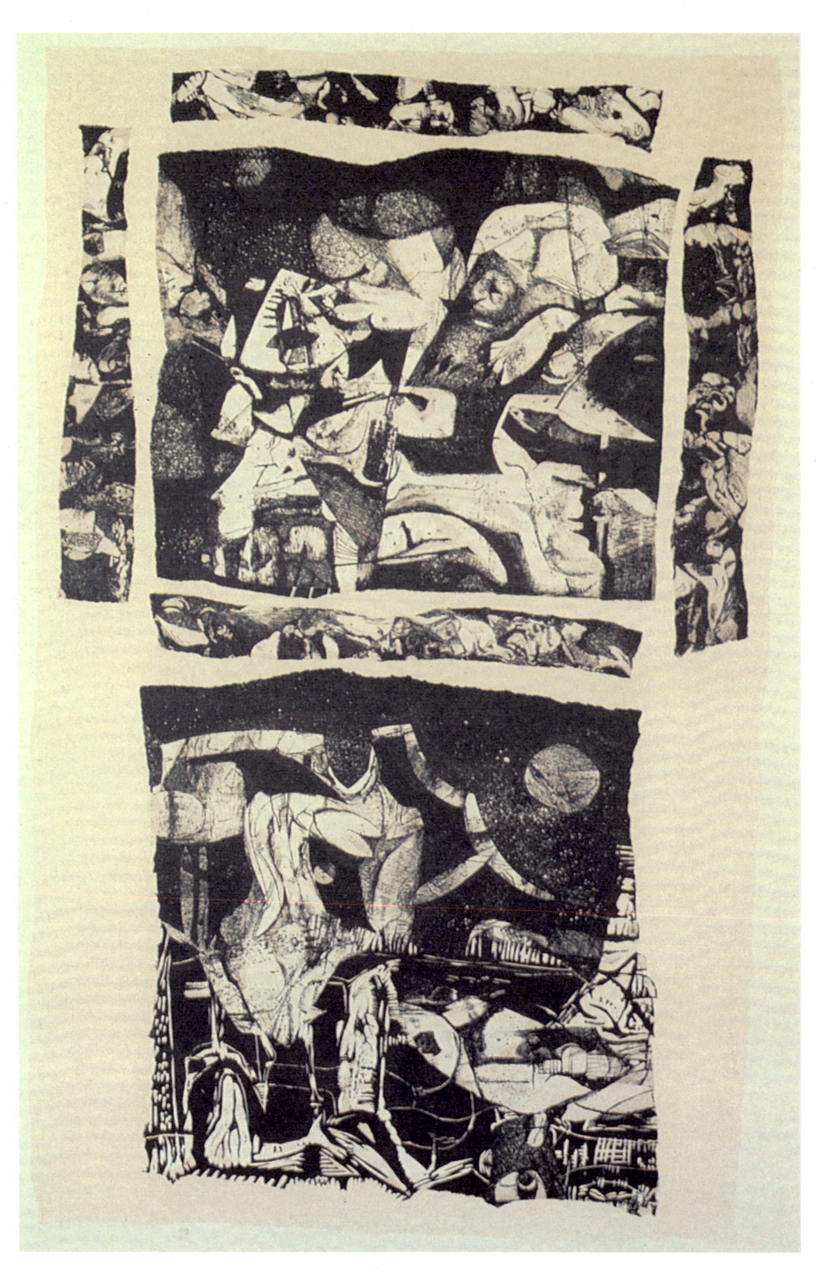

Space Probe, 1973, lithograph and screenprint, 62 x 38

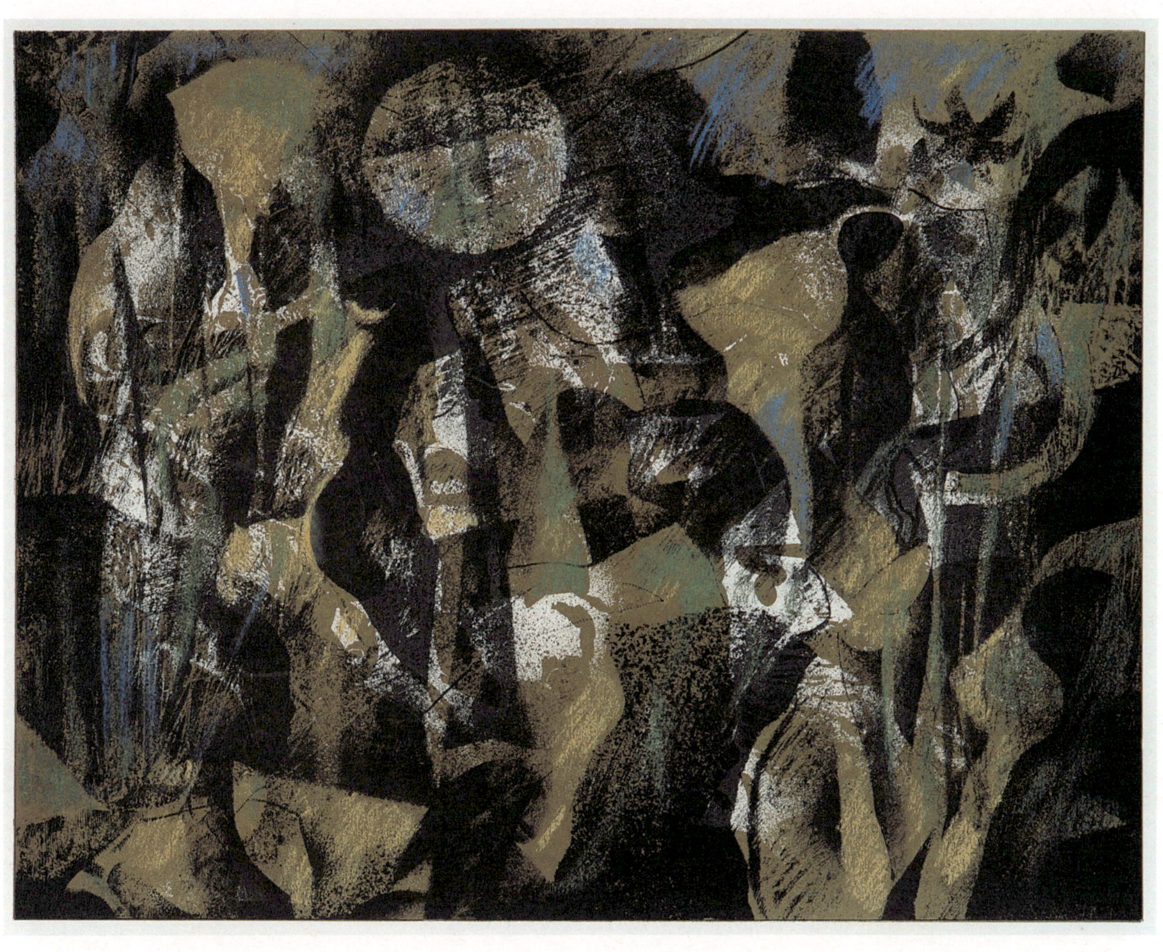

Figuration at Night, 1974, lithograph with hand colour, 52 x 41

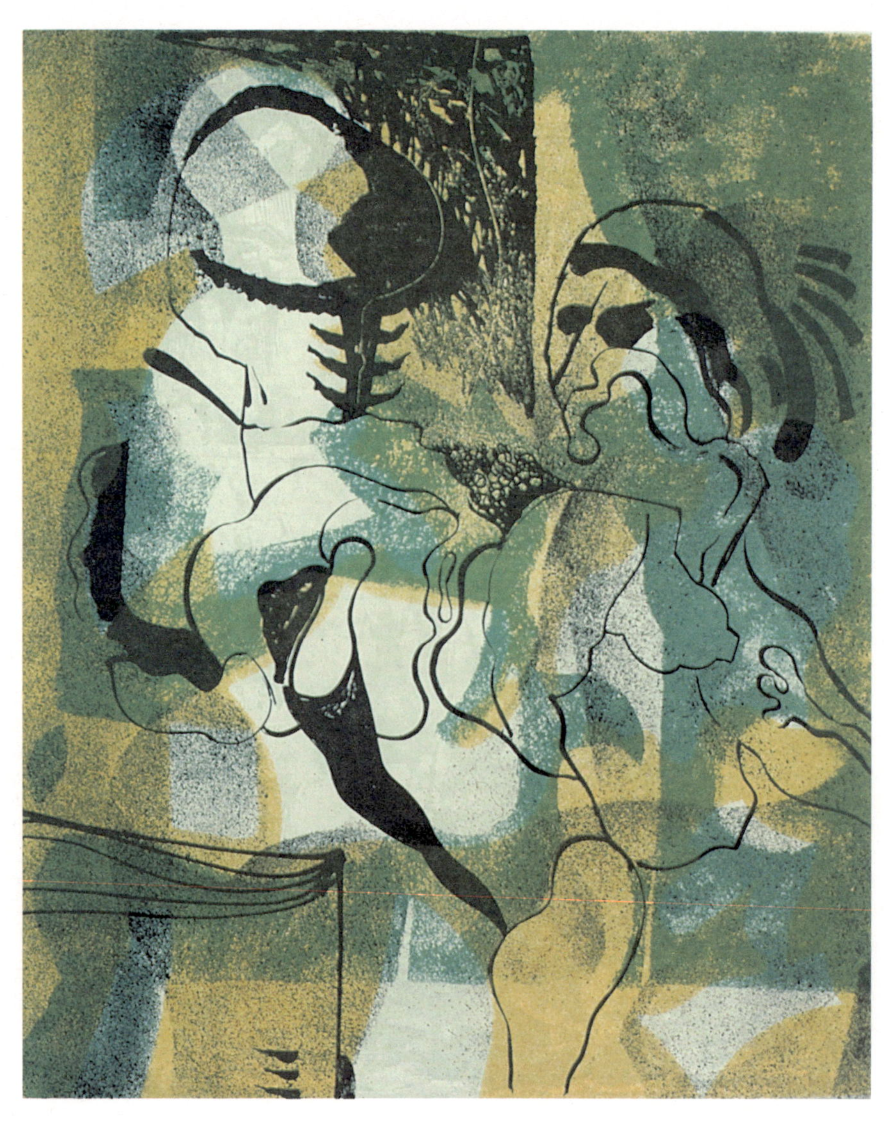

Totentanz, 1975, lithograph, 50 x 40

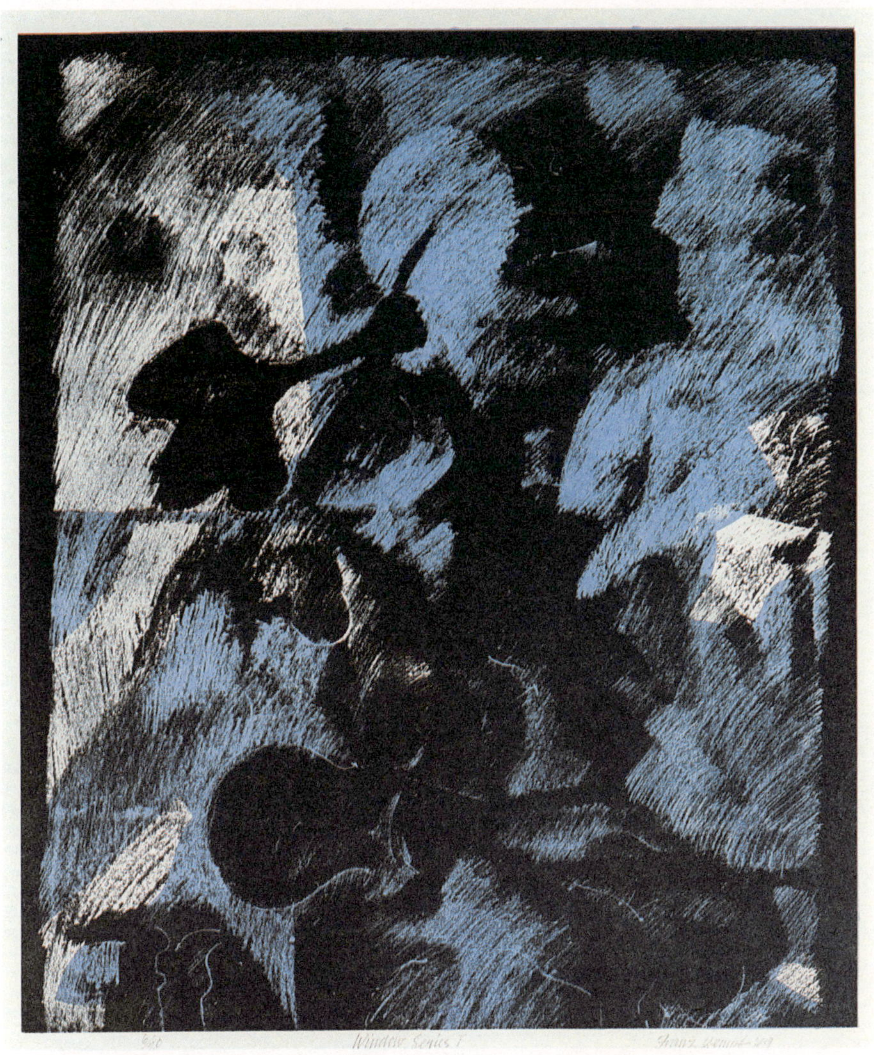

Window Series I, 1979, lithograph, 60.5 x 51

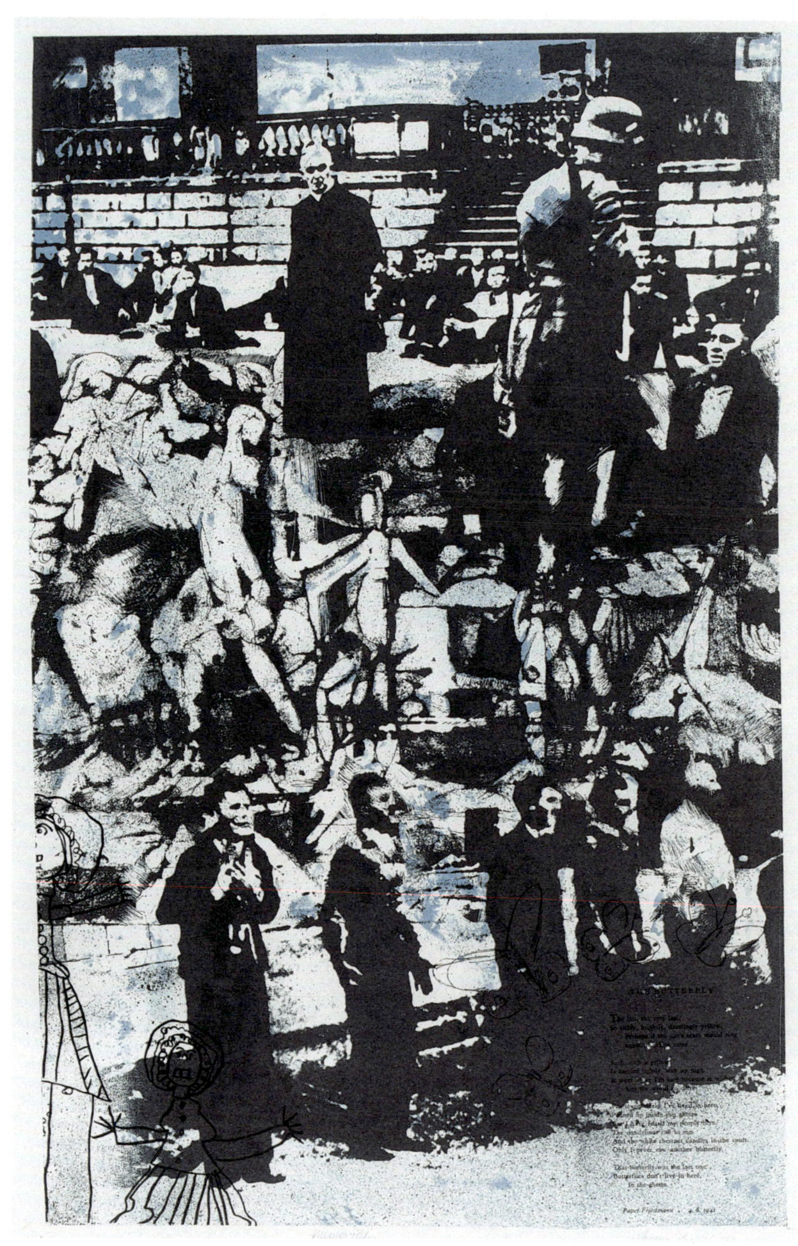

Memorial I,

1979, lithograph, 62.5 x 38.5

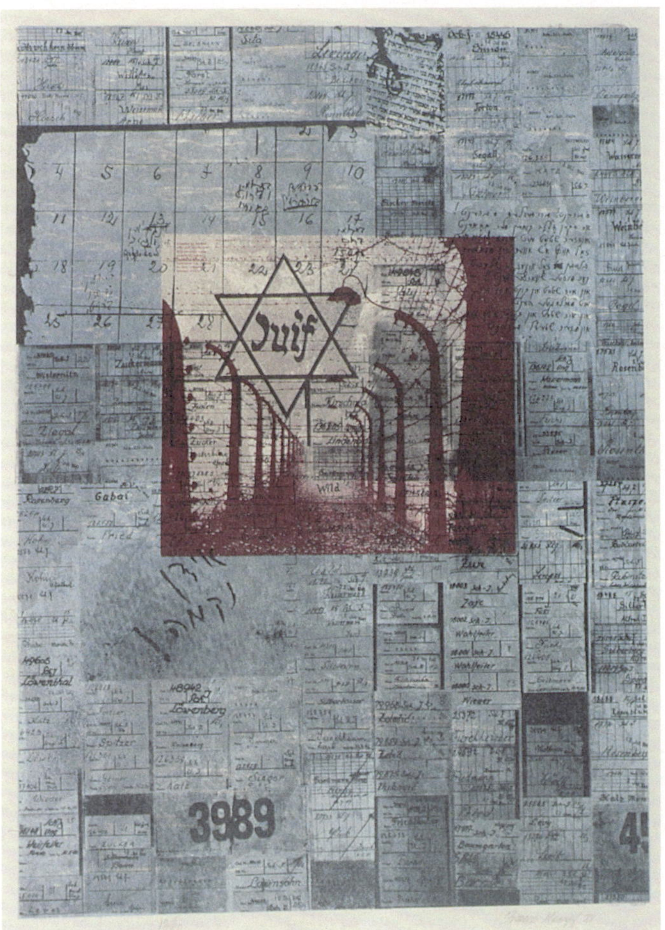

Memorial II,

1981, lithograph, 71 x 50

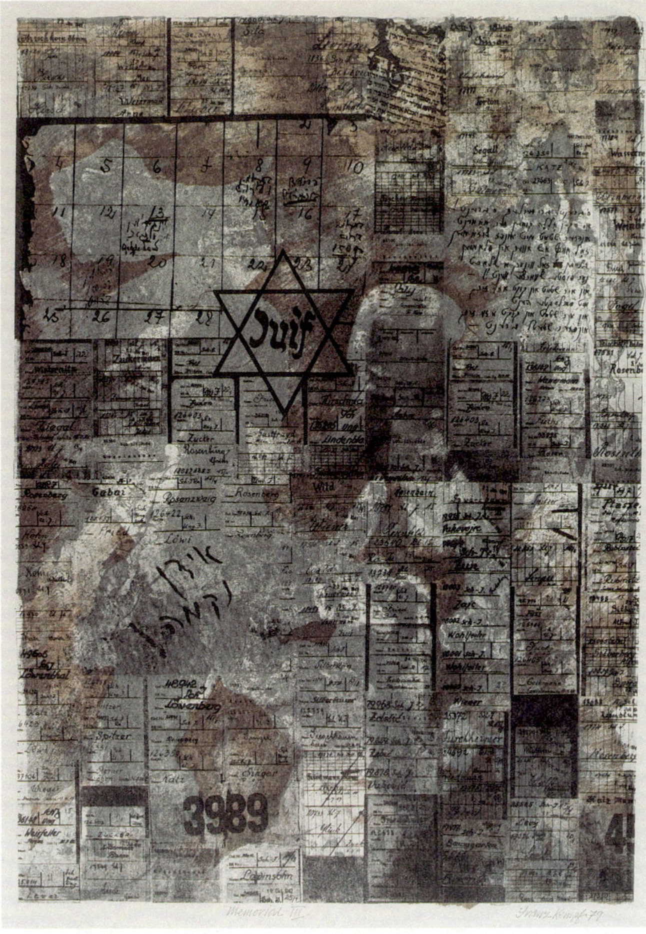

Memorial III,

1979, lithograph, 71 x 50

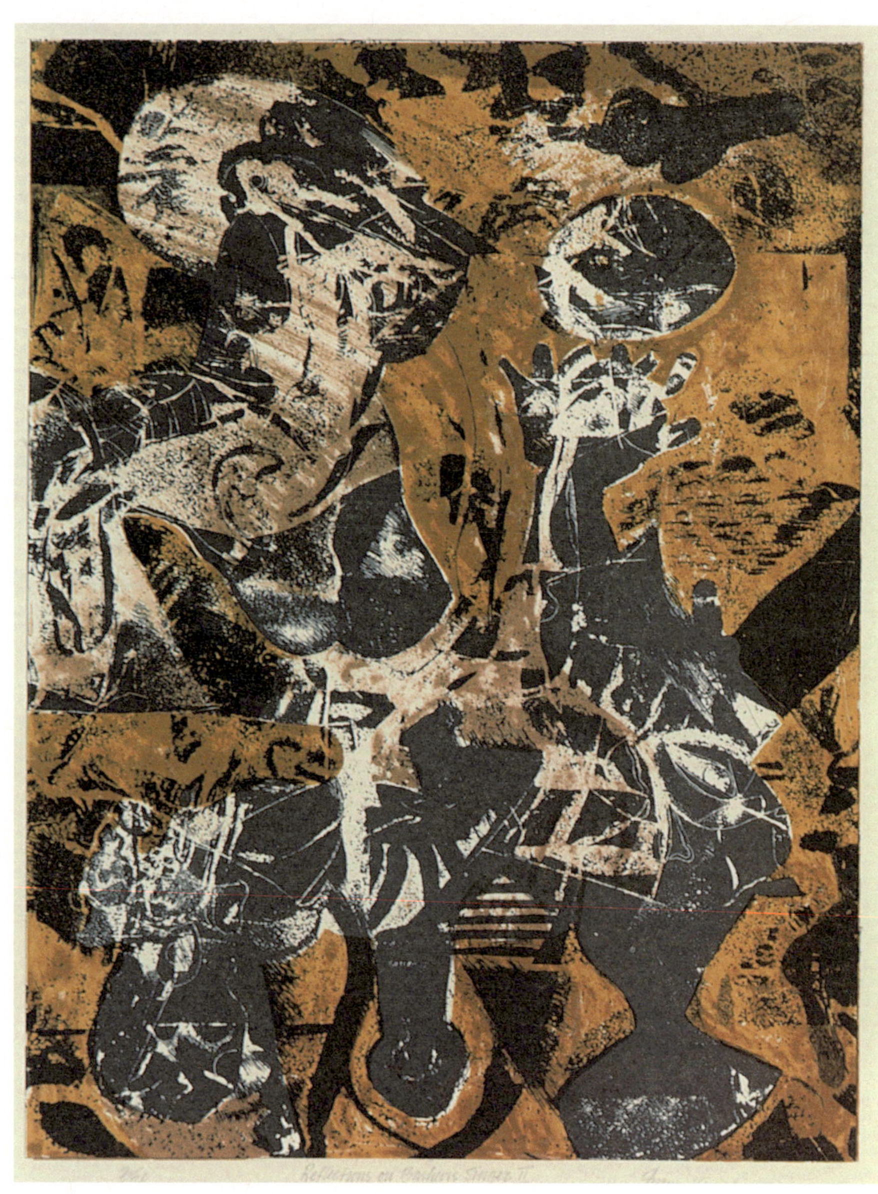

Reflections of Bashevis Singer, 1979, lithograph, 48 x 35.5

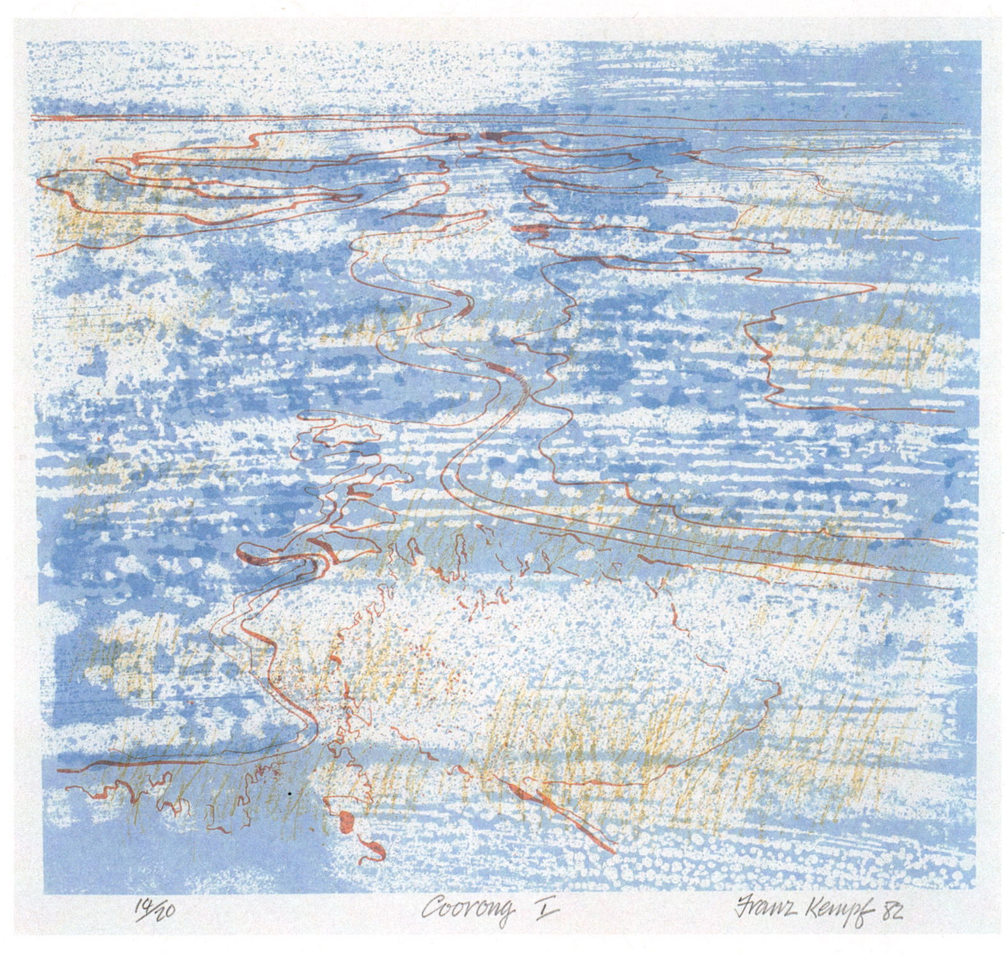

Coorong I, 1982, lithograph, 25.5 x 28

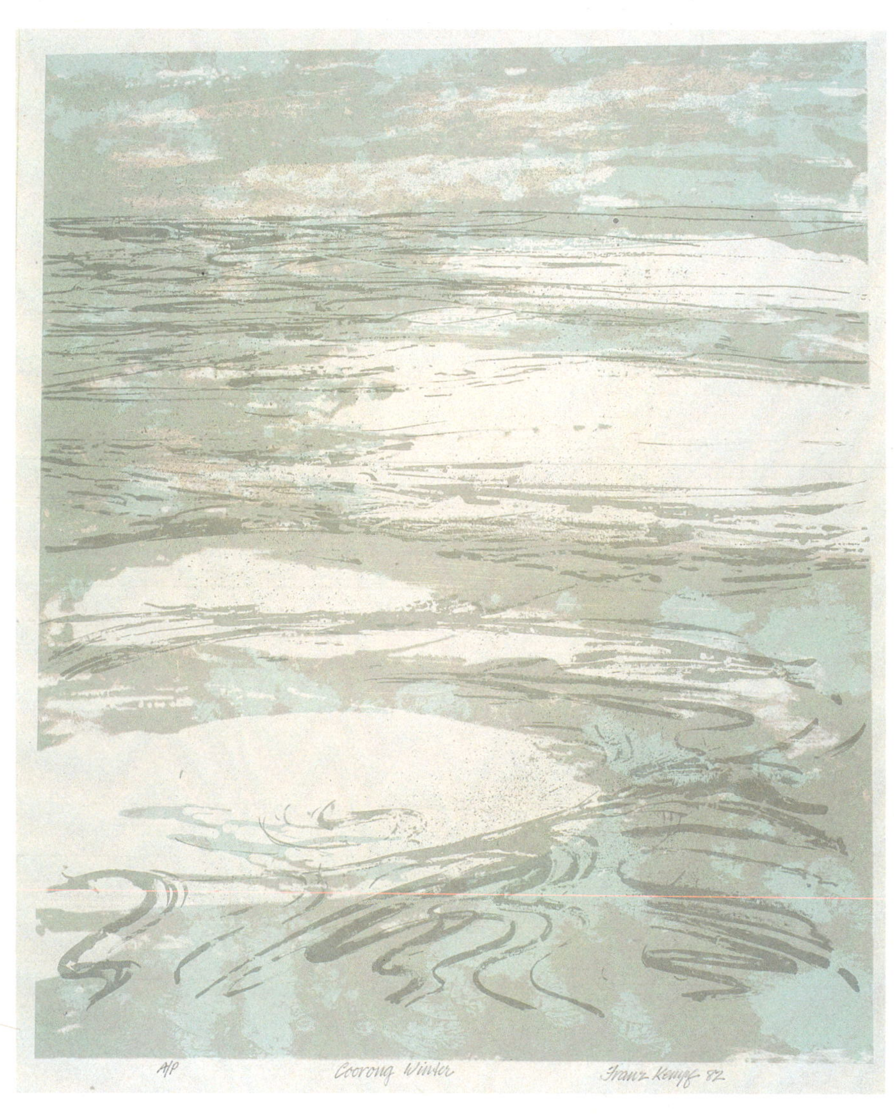

Coorong Winter, *Series*, 1982, lithograph, 62 x 51

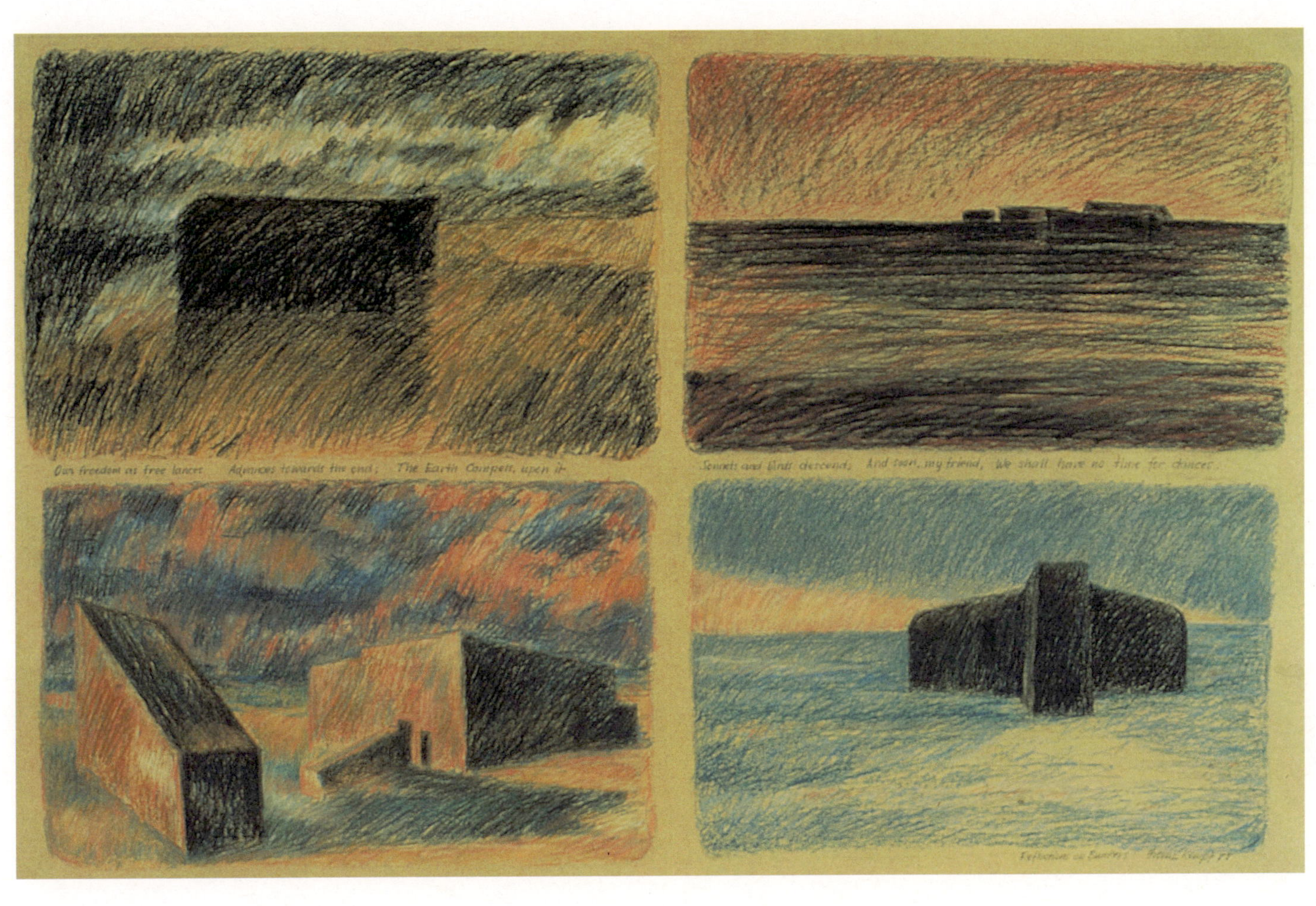

Reflection on Bunkers, 1989, pastel on craft paper, 60 x 91

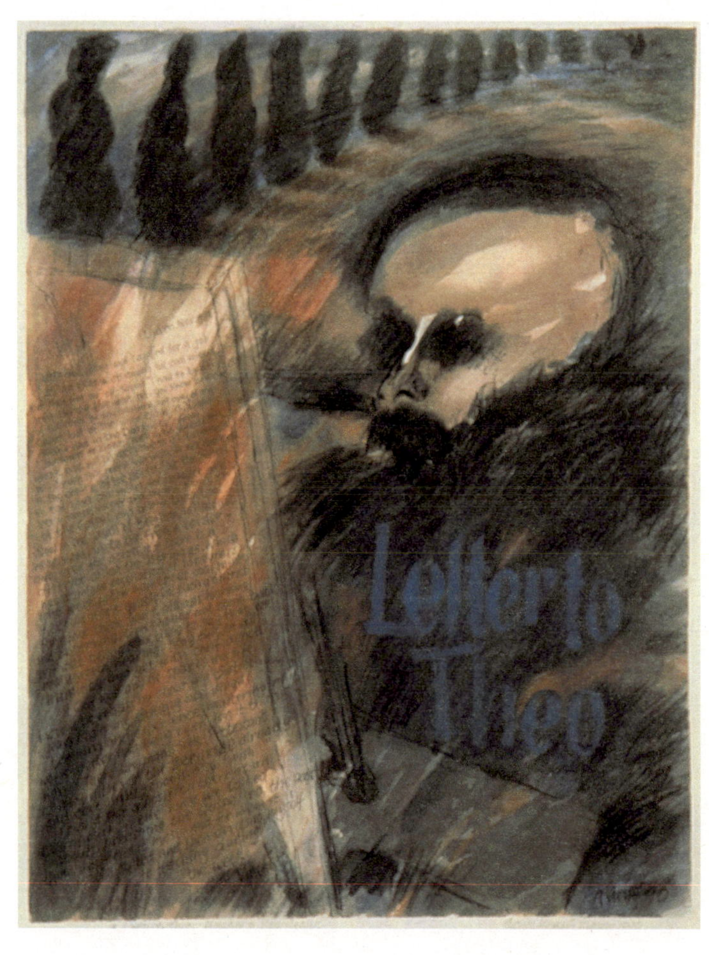

A Letter to Theo, 1990, mixed media on paper, 81 x 60

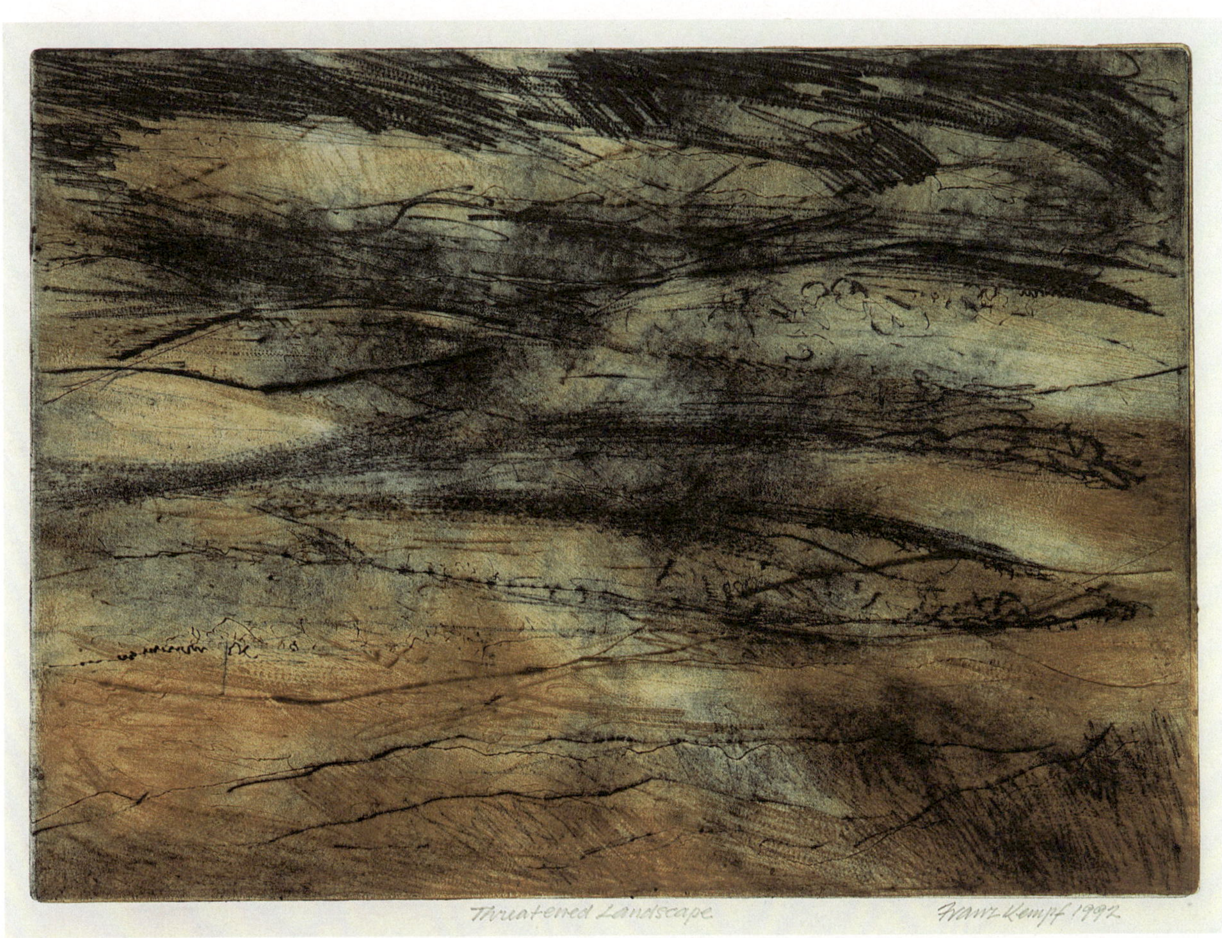

Threatened Landscape, 1992, drypoint, 31 x 42.5

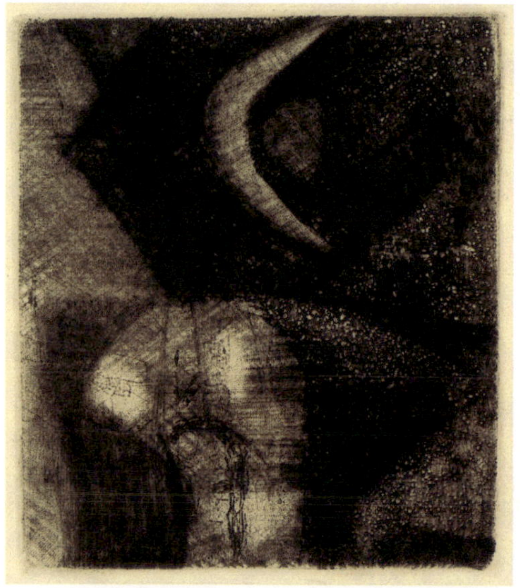

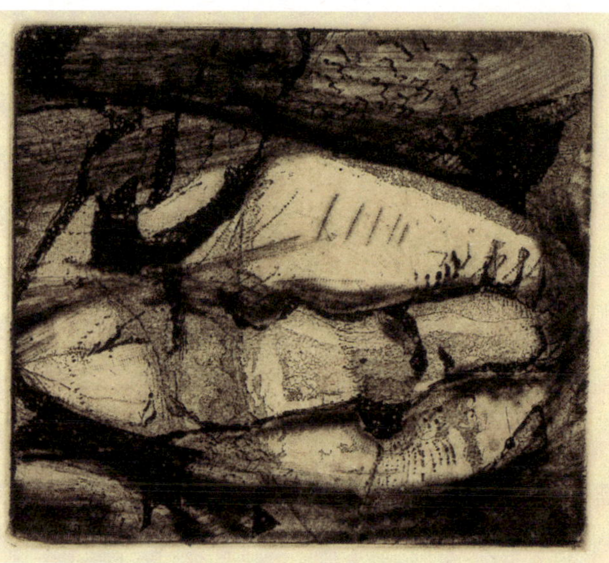

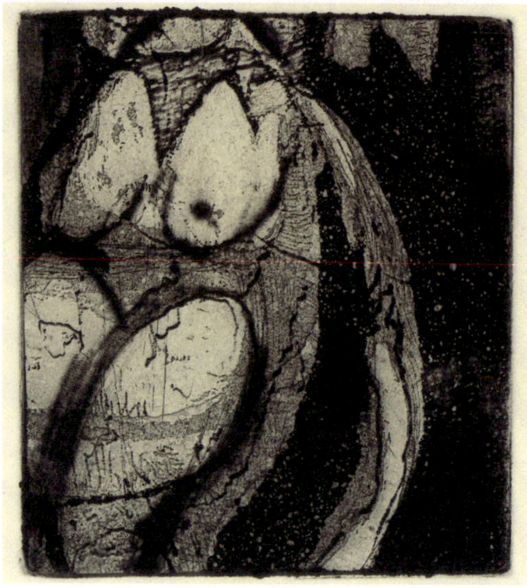

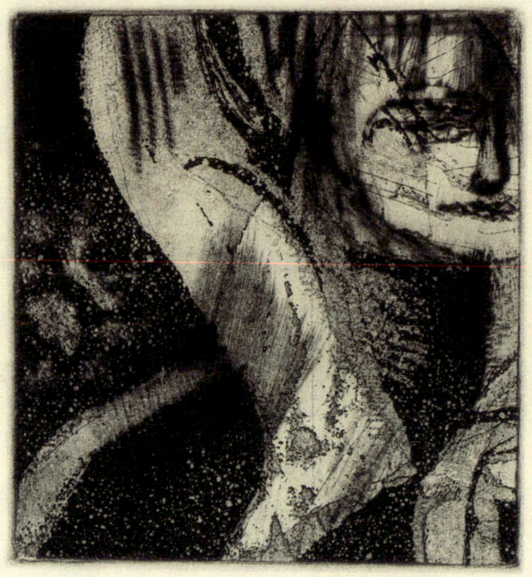

Blessing of the Moon,
1992, aquatint and drypoint, 8 x 7

Night Piece,
1992, aquatint and drypoint, 7 x 8

Figuration and Factory,
1992, aquatint and drypoint, 8 x 7

Performance,
1992, aquatint and drypoint, 8 x 7

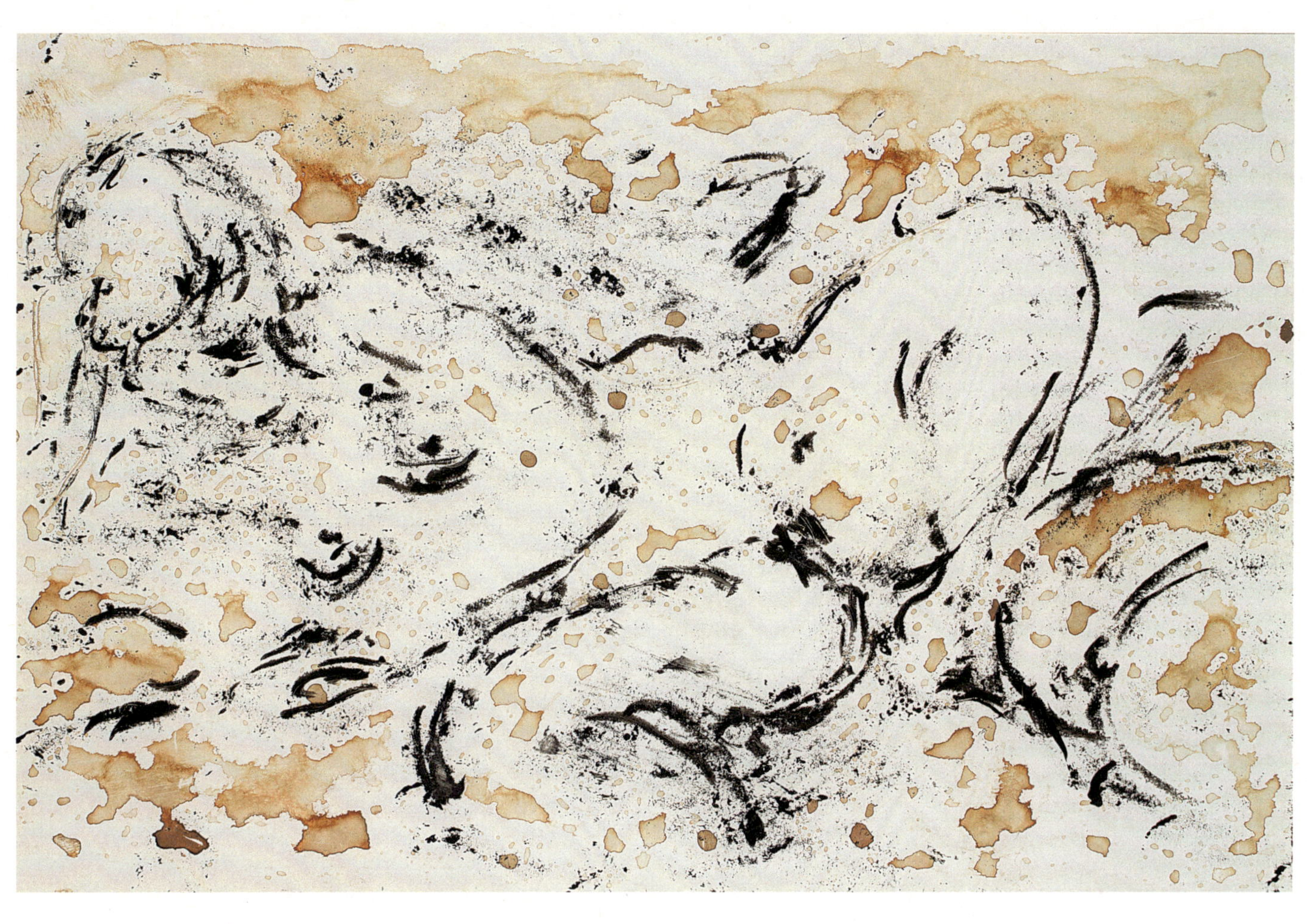

Nude in Repose, 1994, monotype, 12.5 x 19

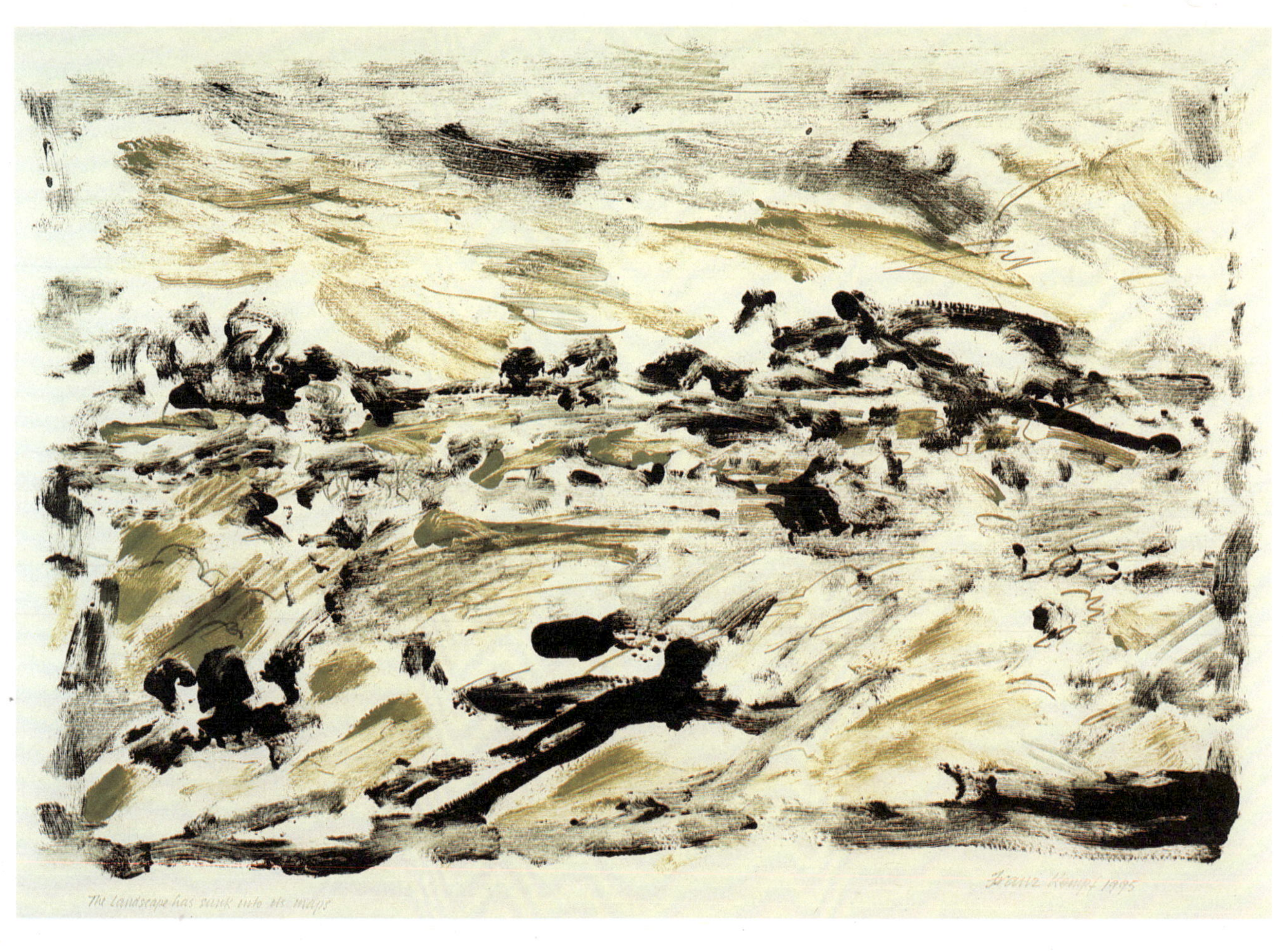

The Landscape Has Sunk into its Maps, 1995, monoprint, 49 x 71

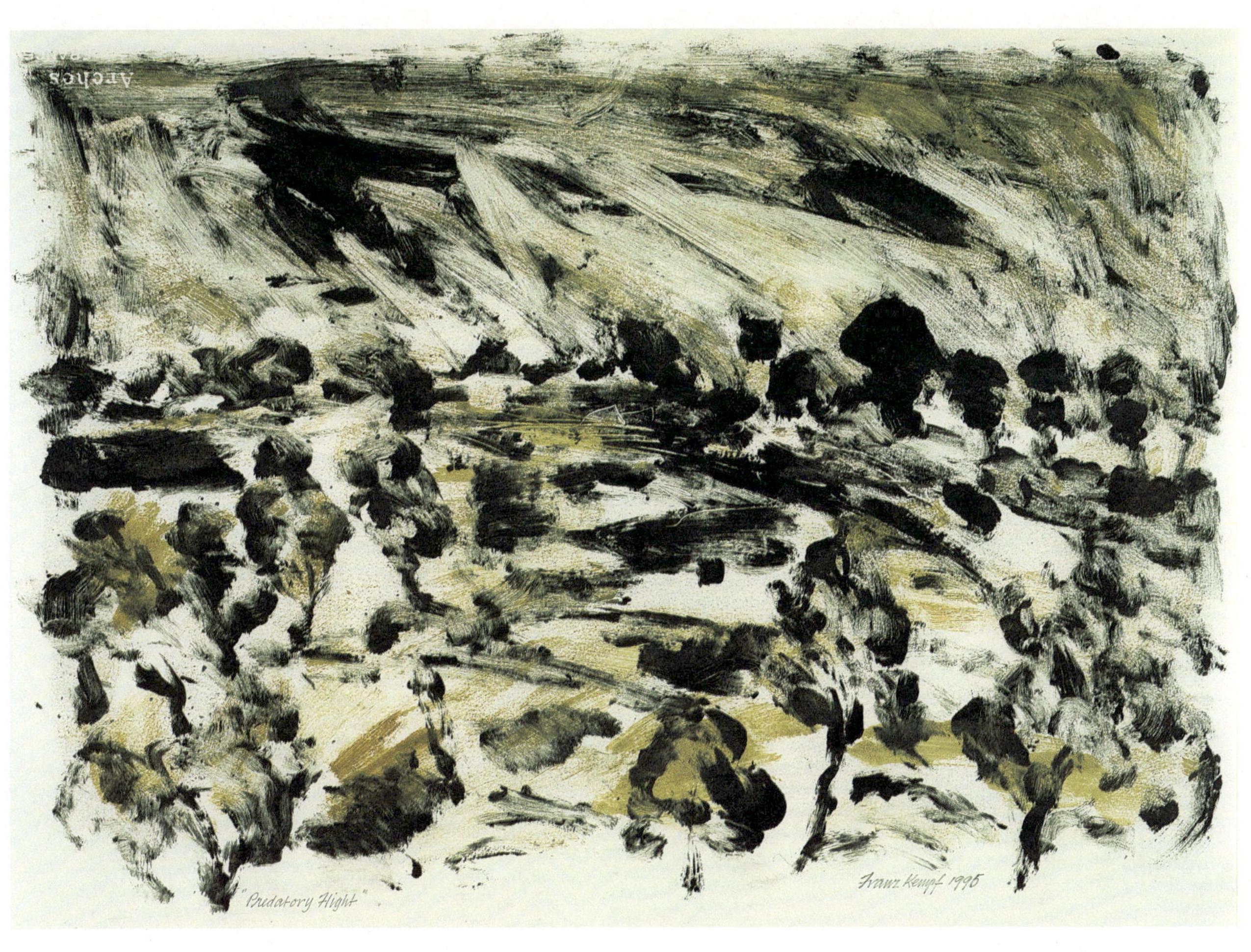

Predatory Flight, 1995, monotype, 57 x 76

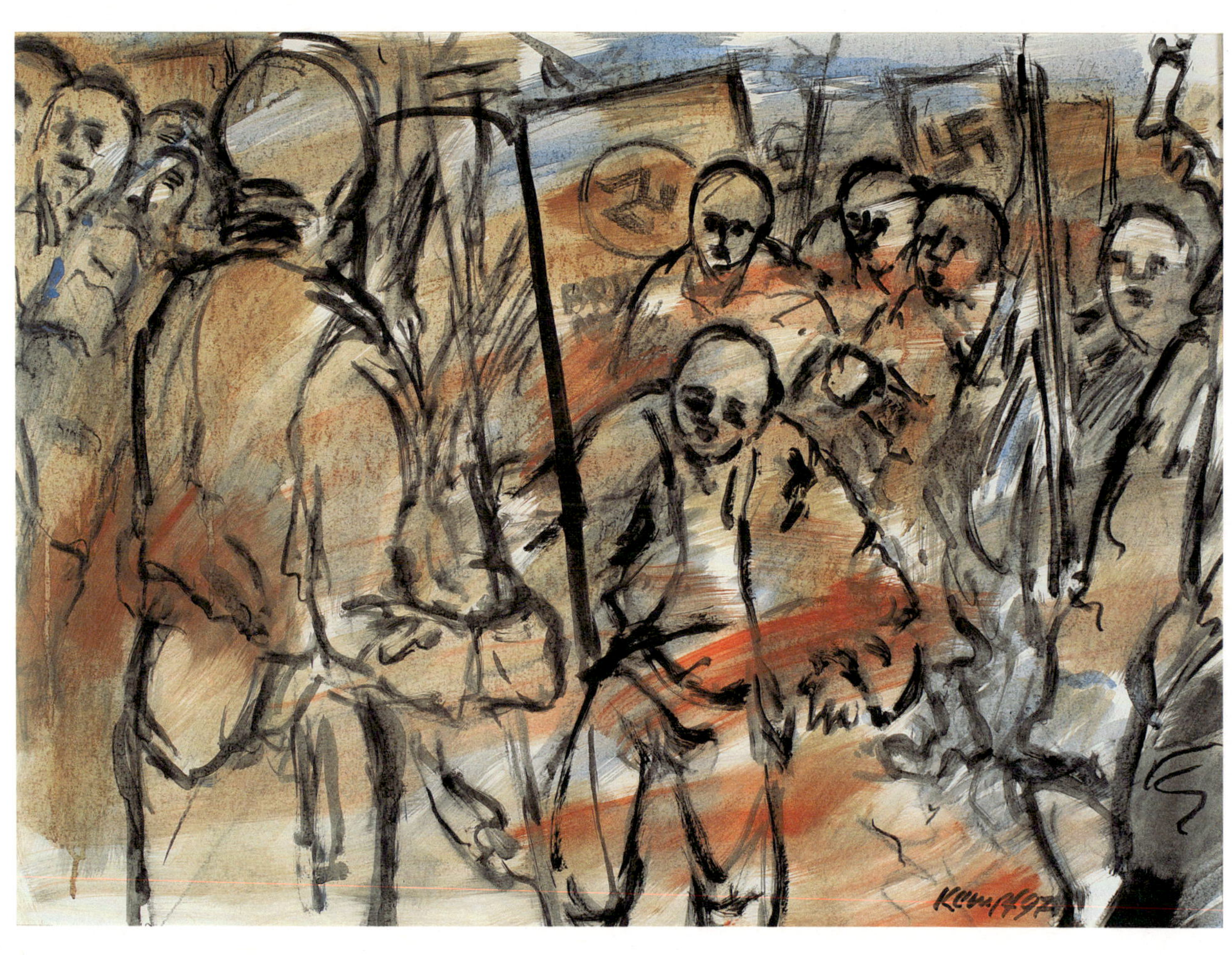

Don't Mess With White Power, 1997, oil on paper, 56 x 76

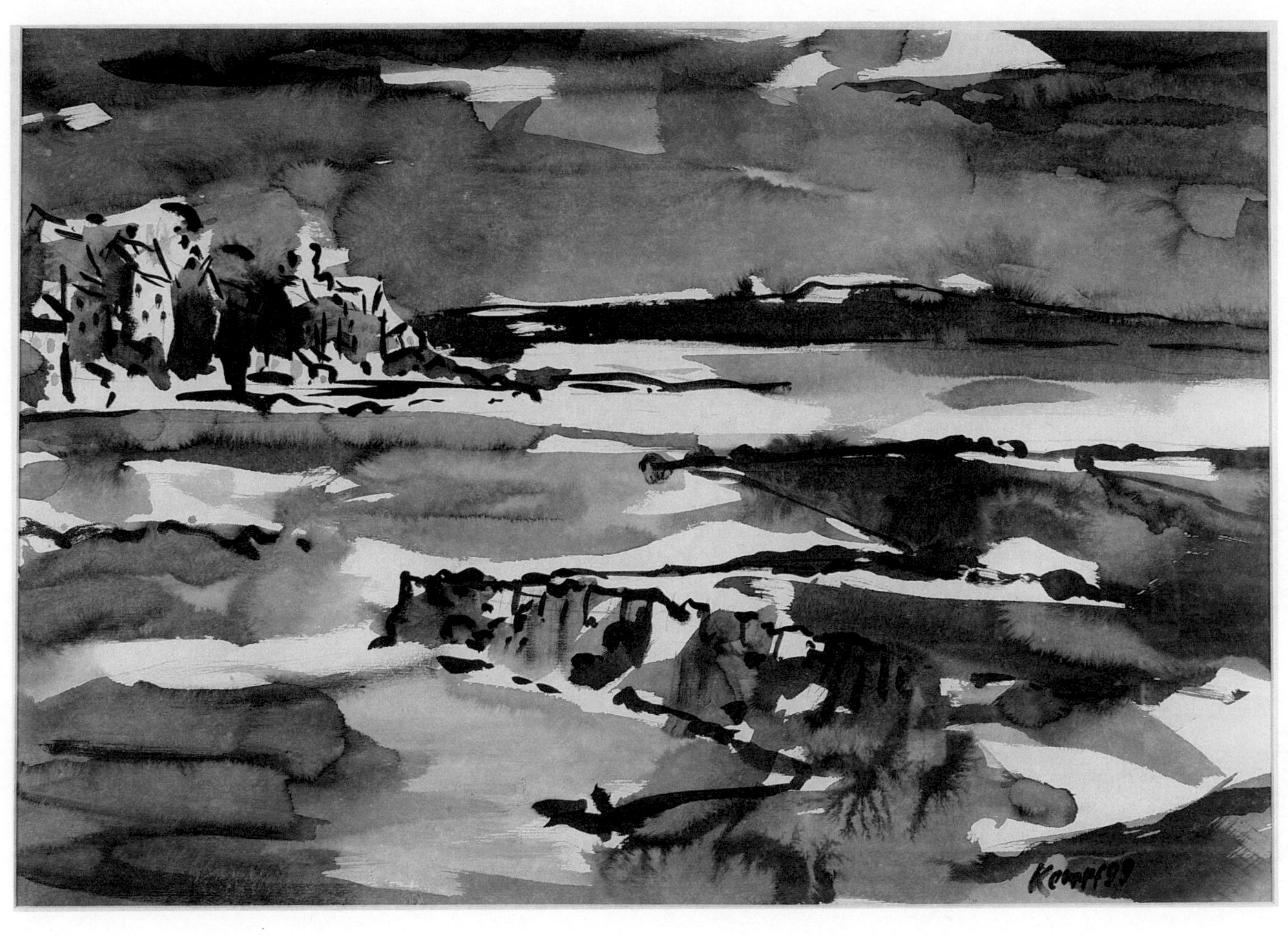

Winter Waters Devon I, 1999, Chinese ink drawing, 62 x 90

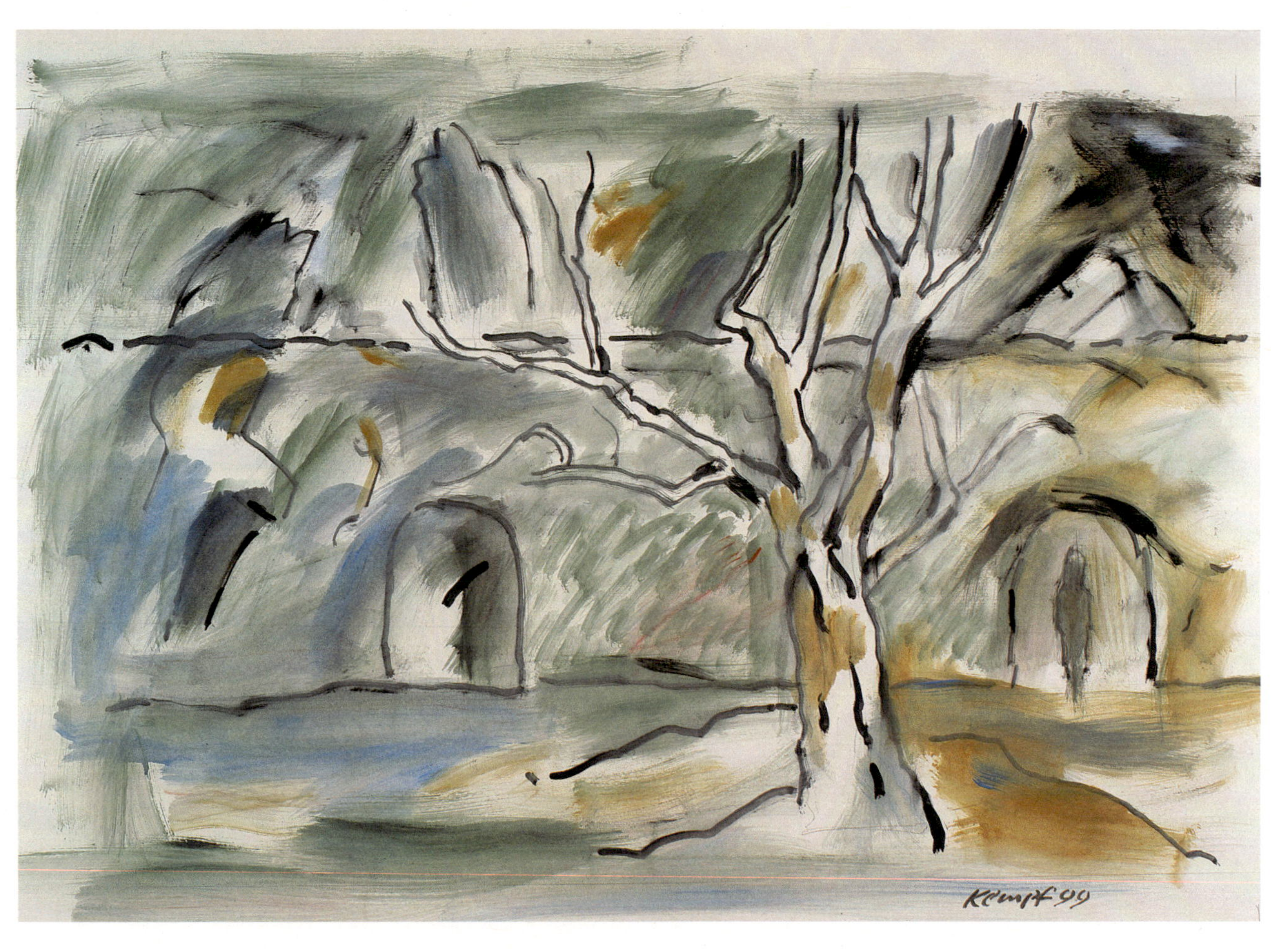

A Silent Garden, 1999, mixed media on paper, 54 x 82.5

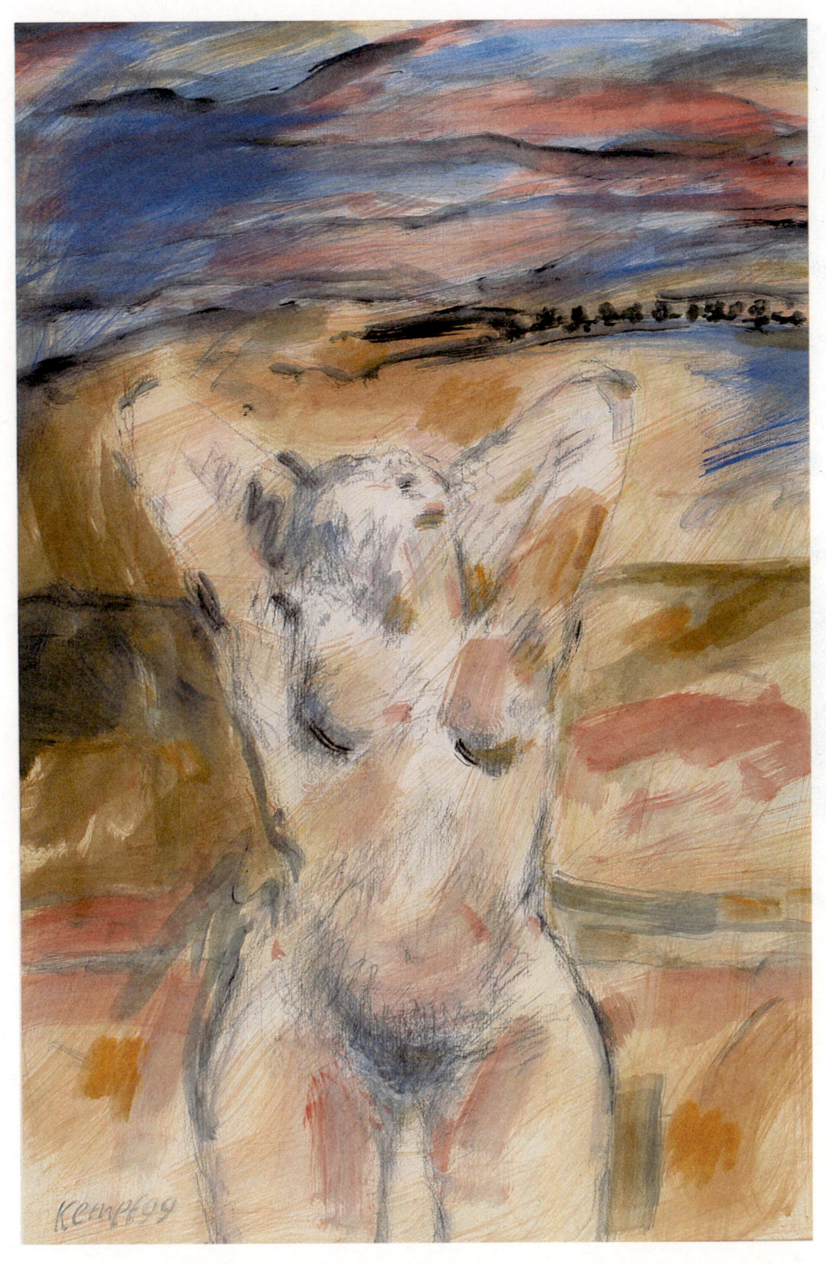

Lamentation I, 1999, mixed media on paper, 86 x 55

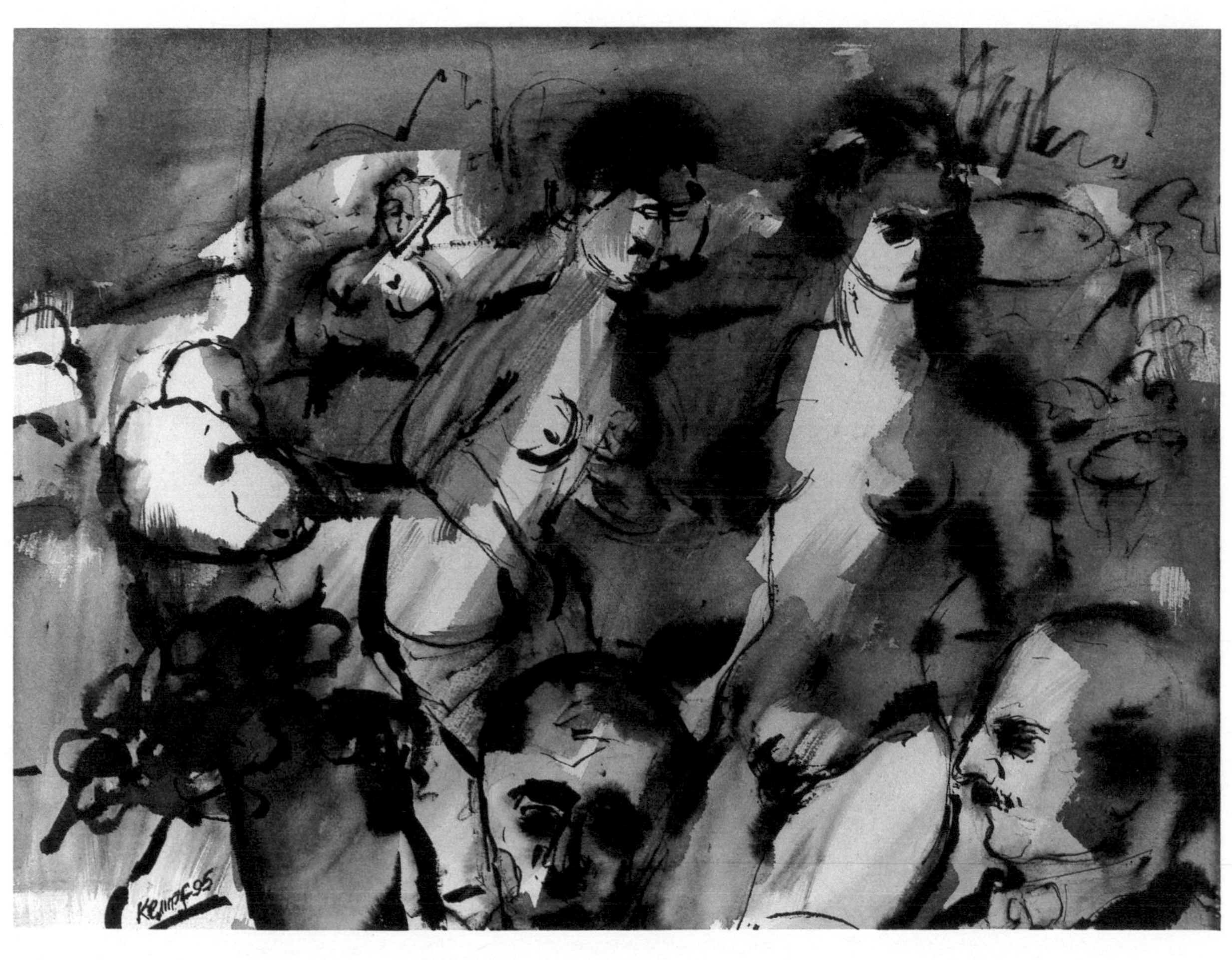

Lunch Time at the Girlie Bar, 1995, Chinese ink and wash, 45 x 57

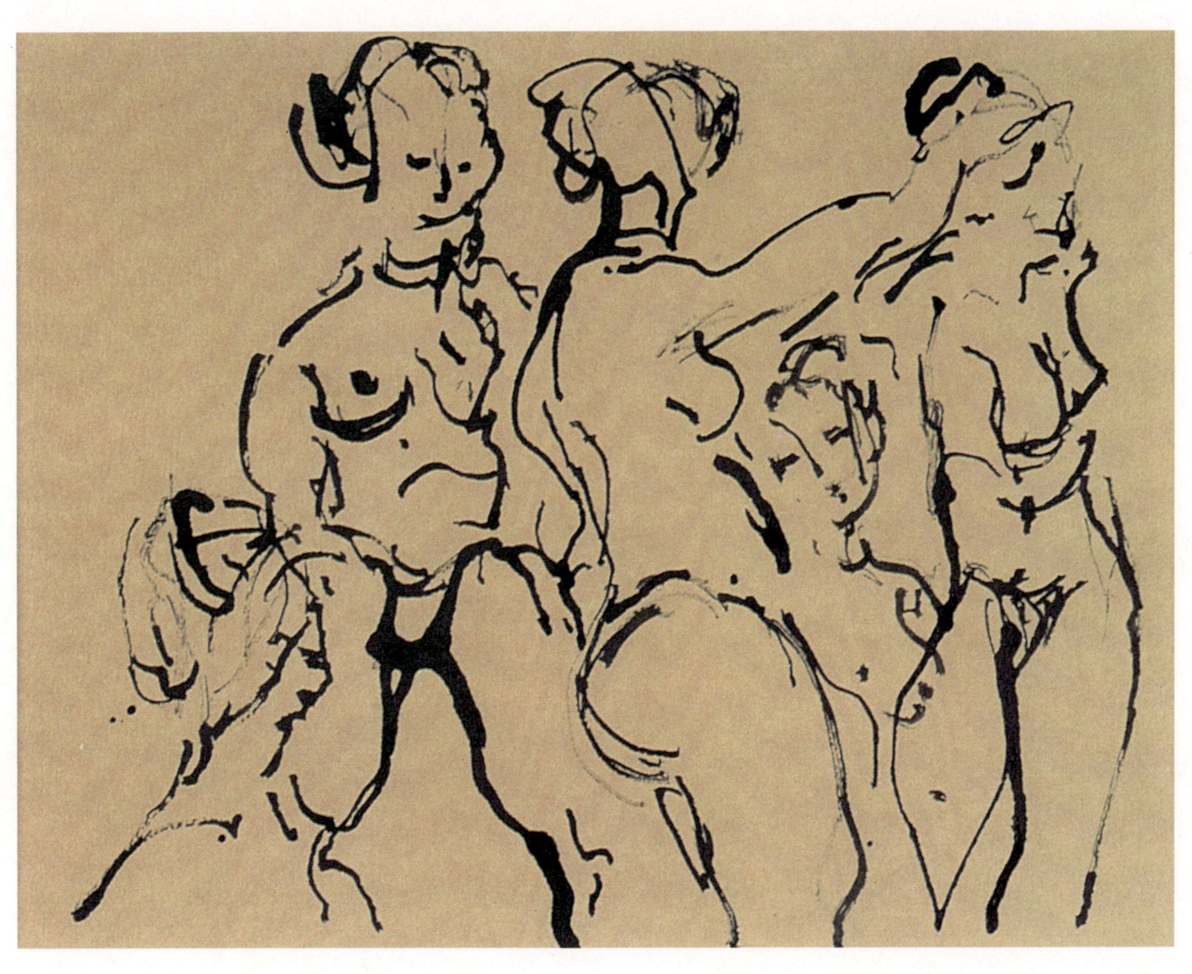

The Chorus, 1999, Chinese ink, 15.5 x 19.5

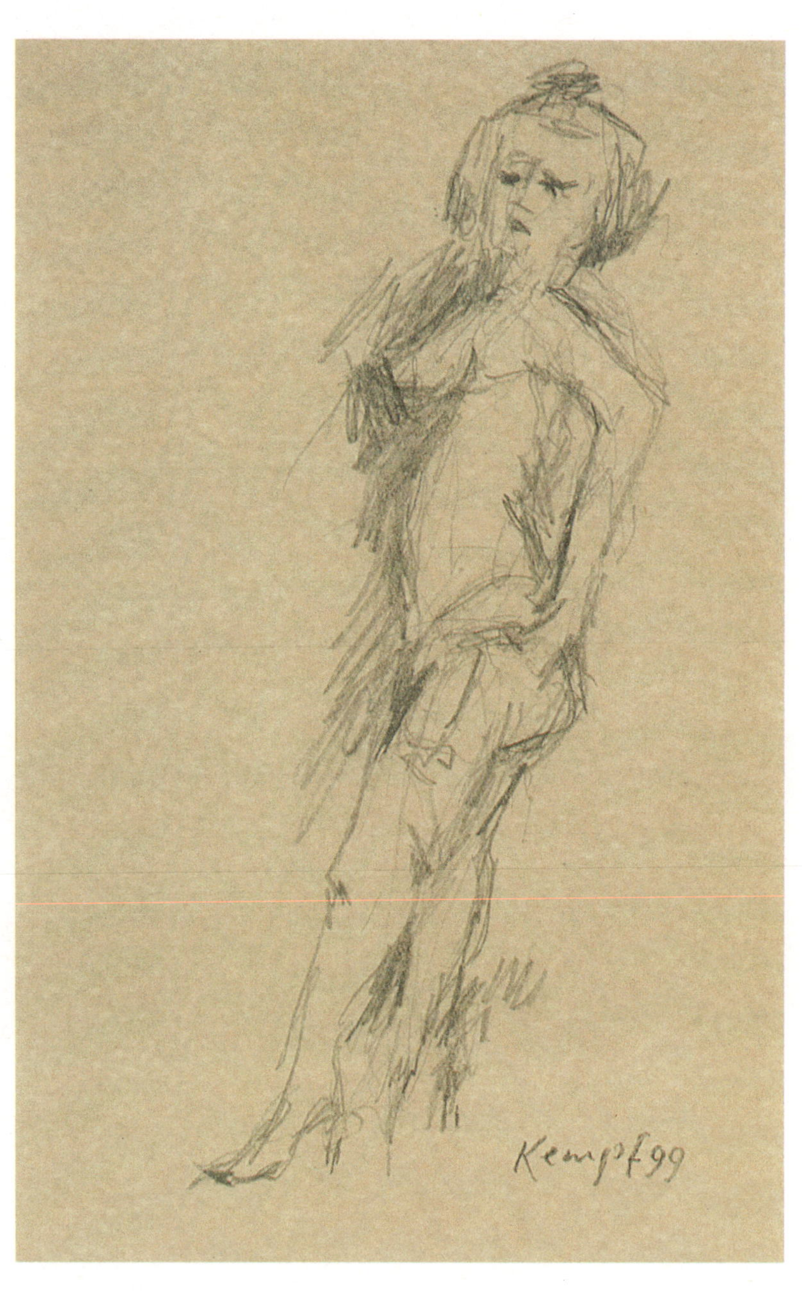

Standing Figure in the Wings, 1999, pencil drawing, 18.5 x 11.5

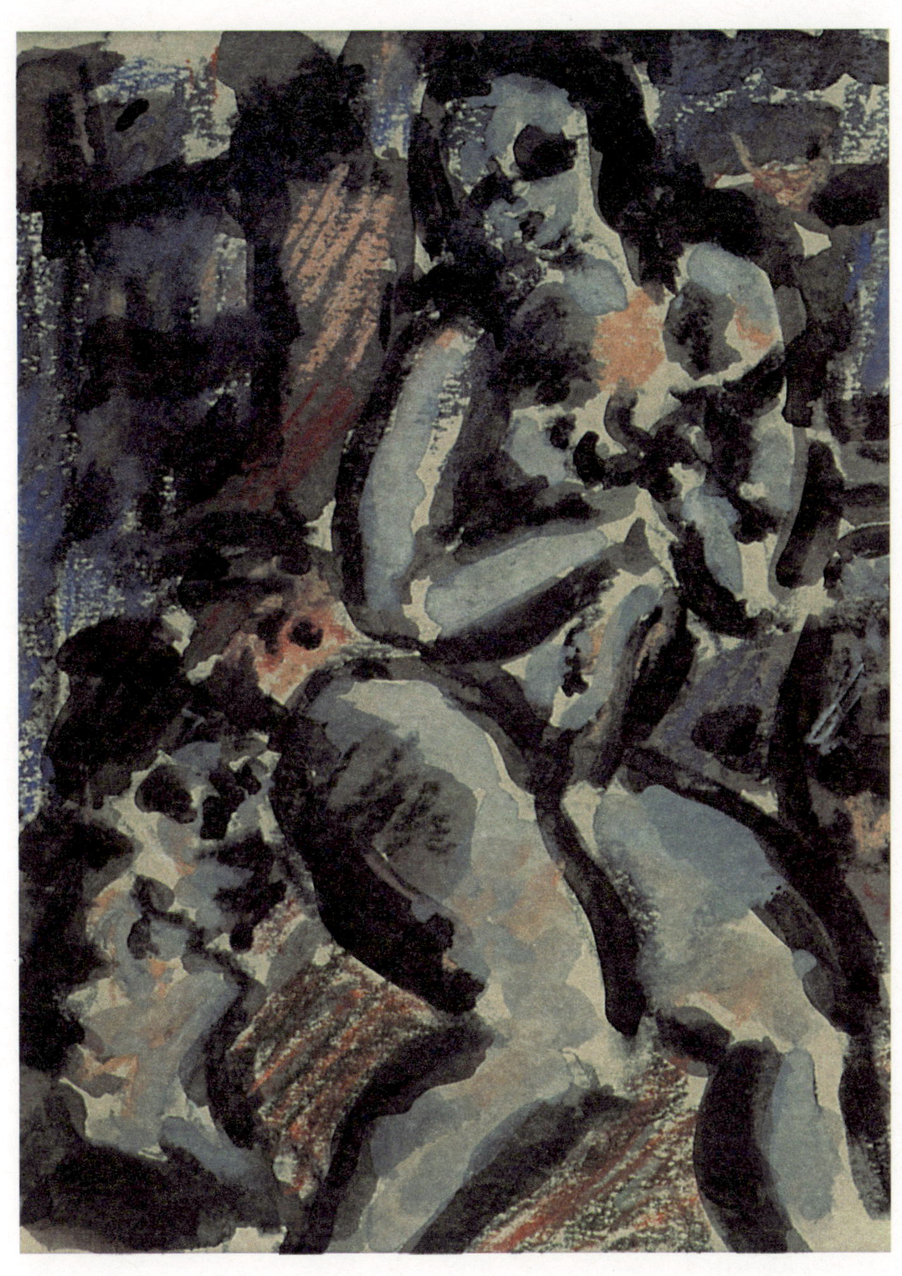

Table Dancer Entertainer, 1999, pastel, 17.5 x 12.5

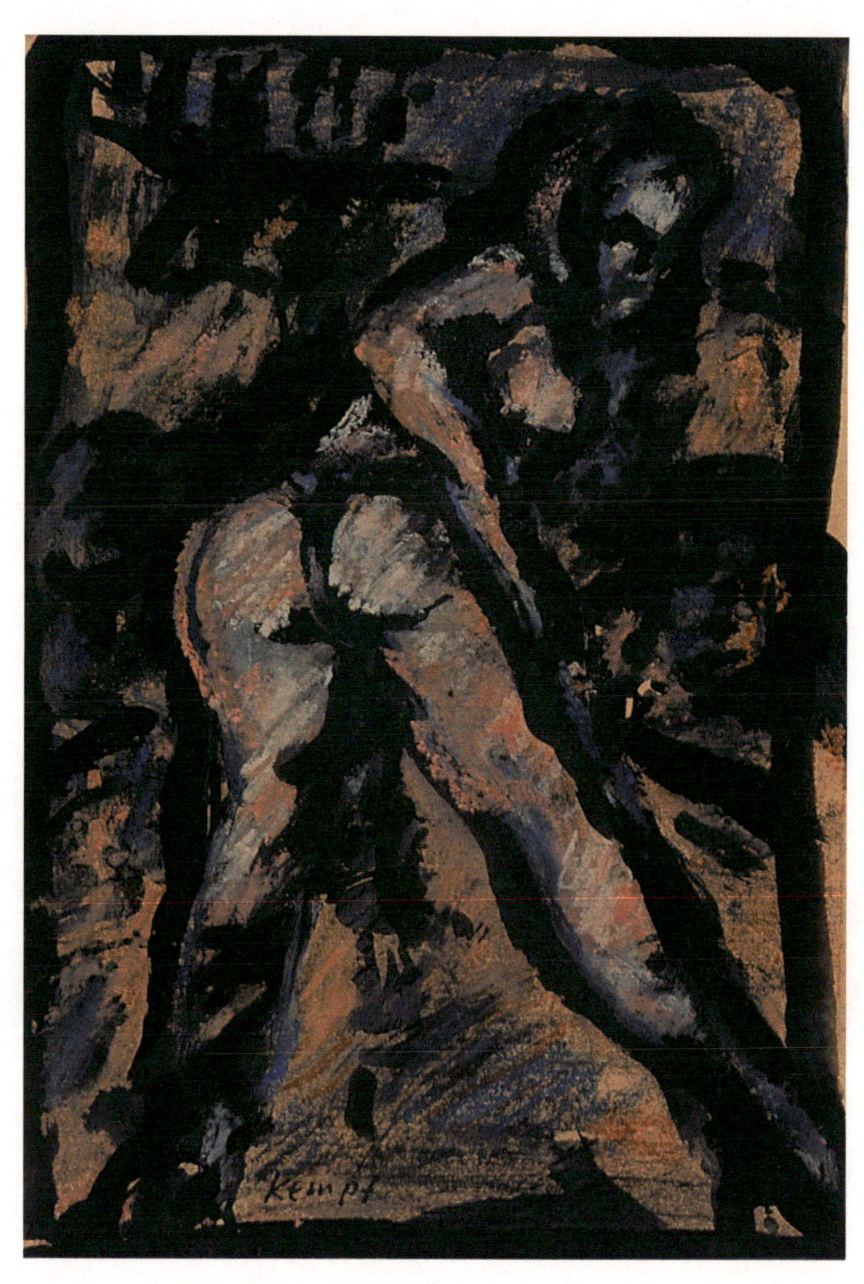

Entertainer, 1999, pastel, 18.5 x 12.5

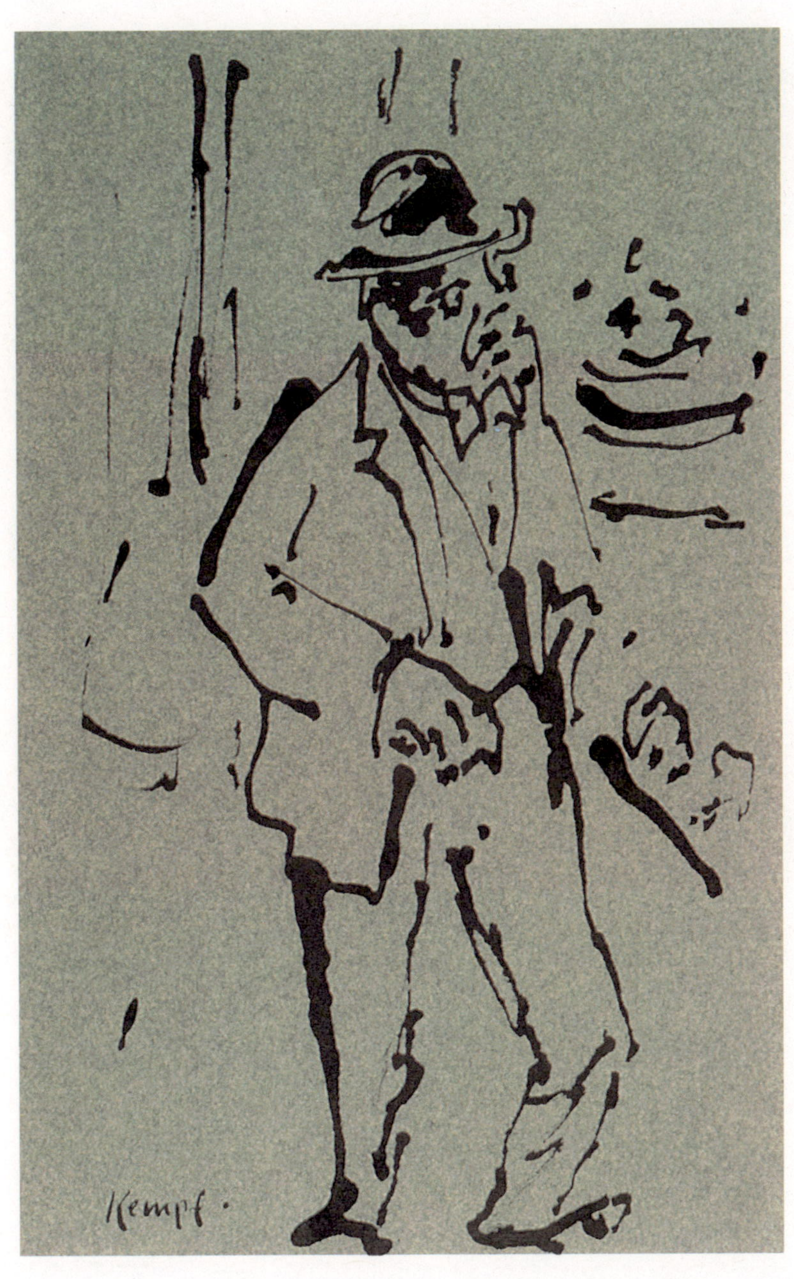

Entrance, 1999, Chinese ink drawing, 19.5 x 12

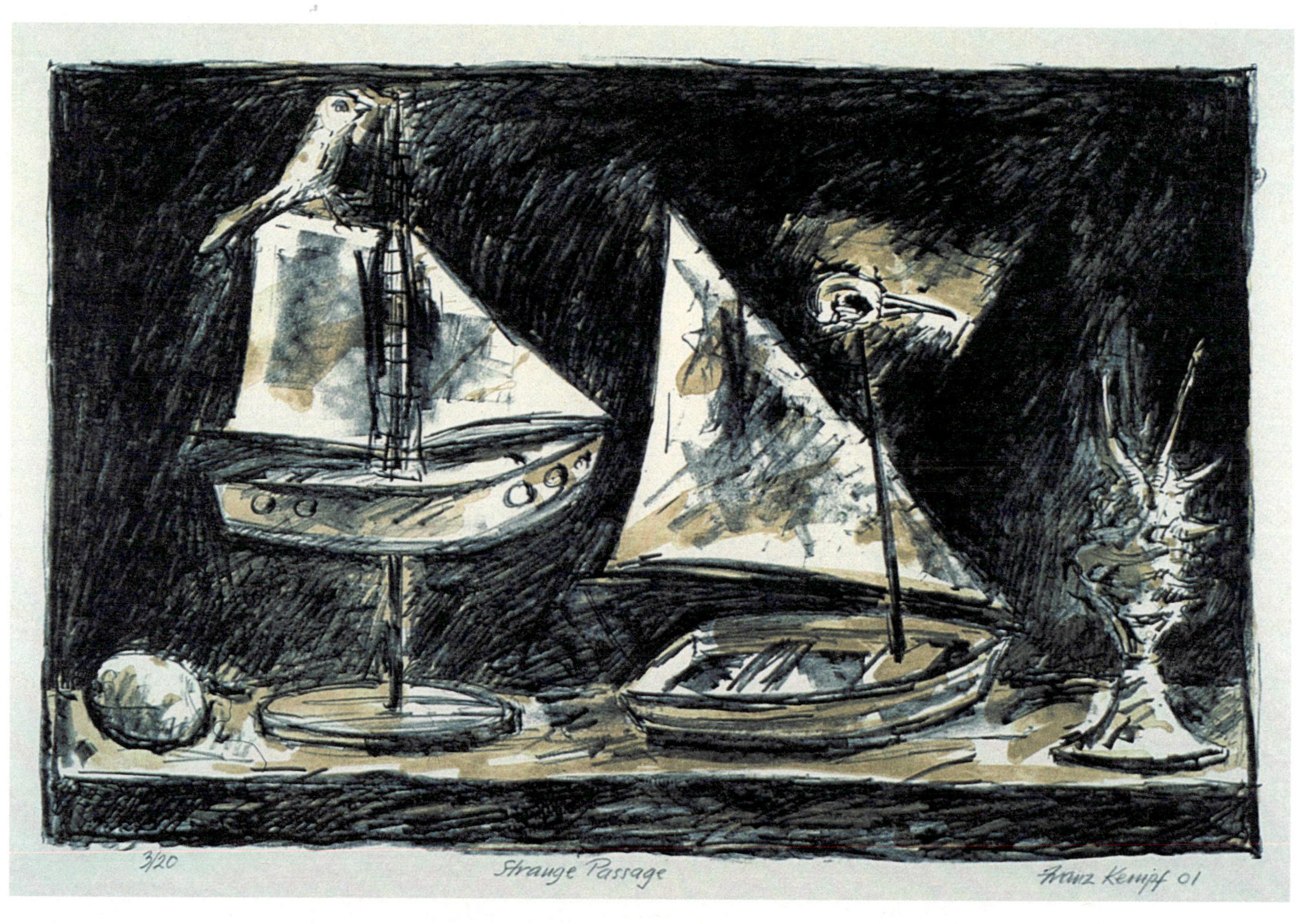

Strange Passage, 2001, lithograph, 38 x 57.5

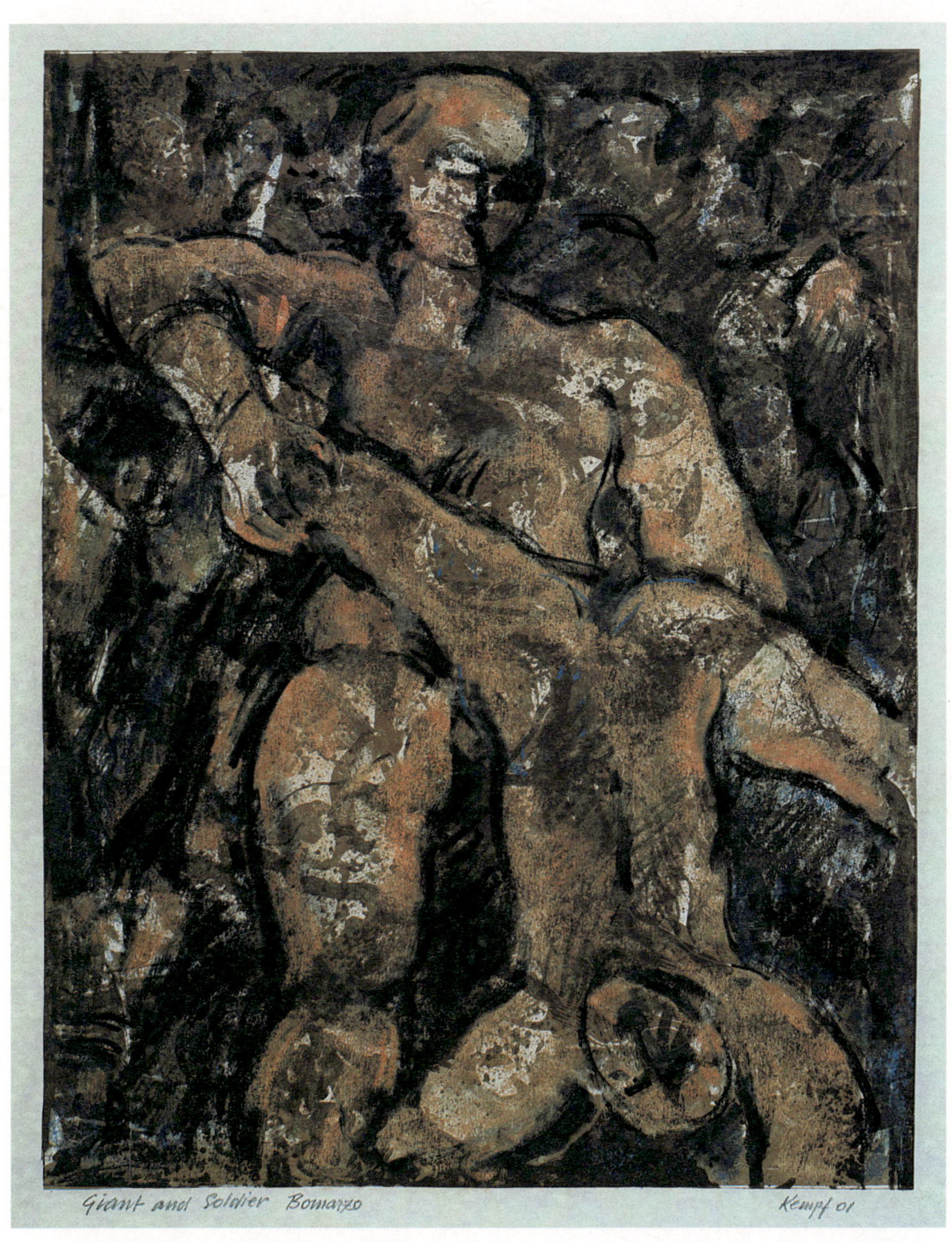

Giant and Soldier – Bomarzo Series, 2001, mixed media on paper, 51 x 39

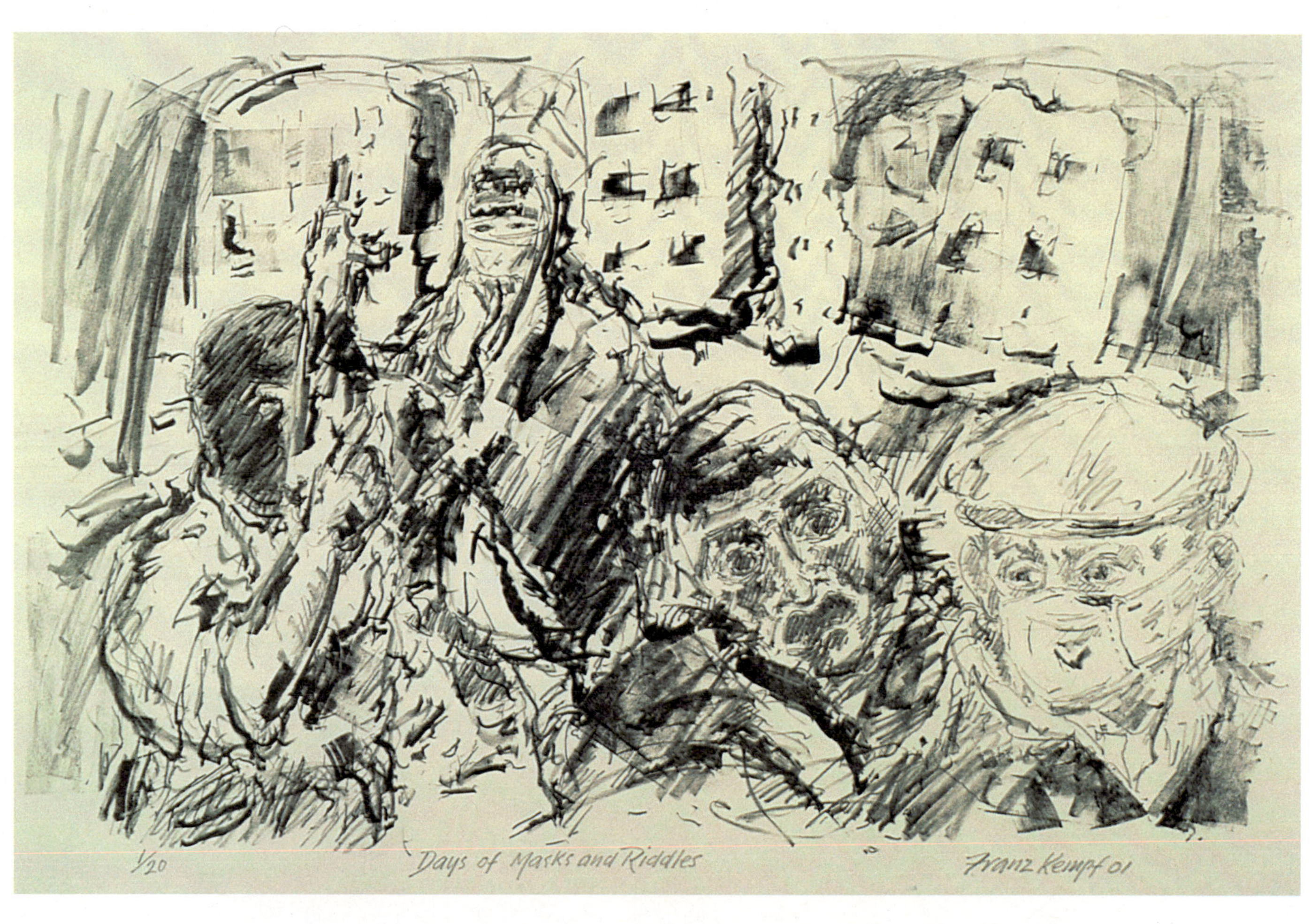

Days of Masks and Riddles, 2001, lithograph, 38 x 57.5

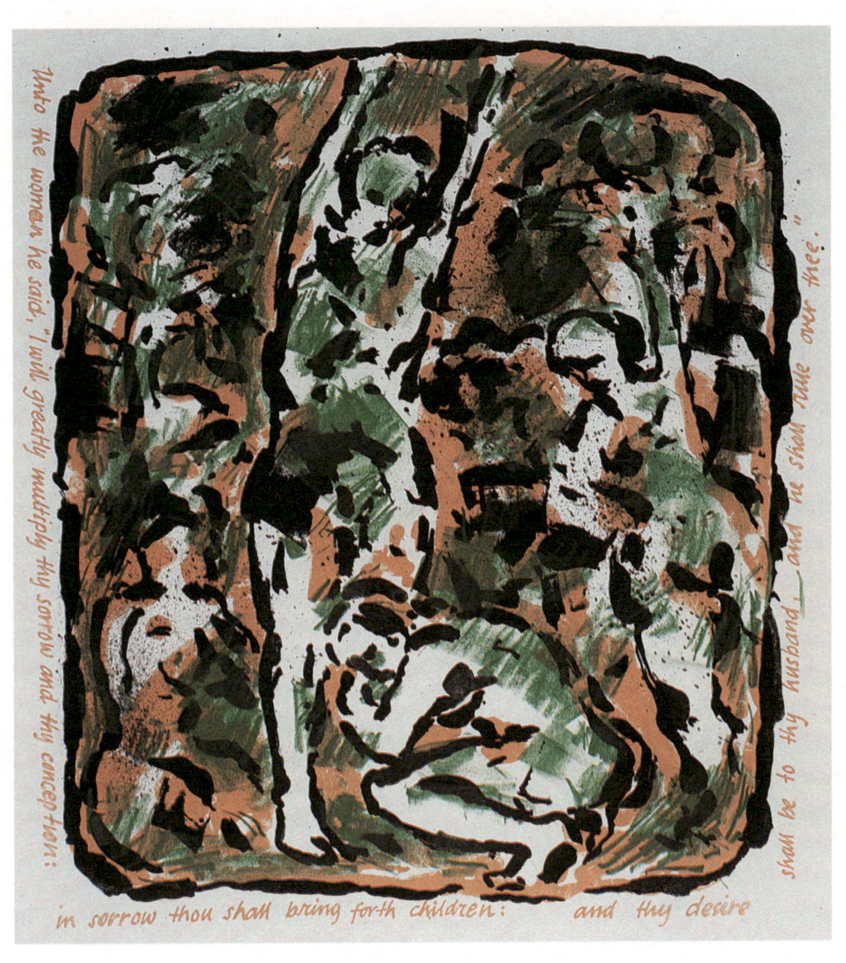

The Garden, 2001, lithograph, 33 x 29

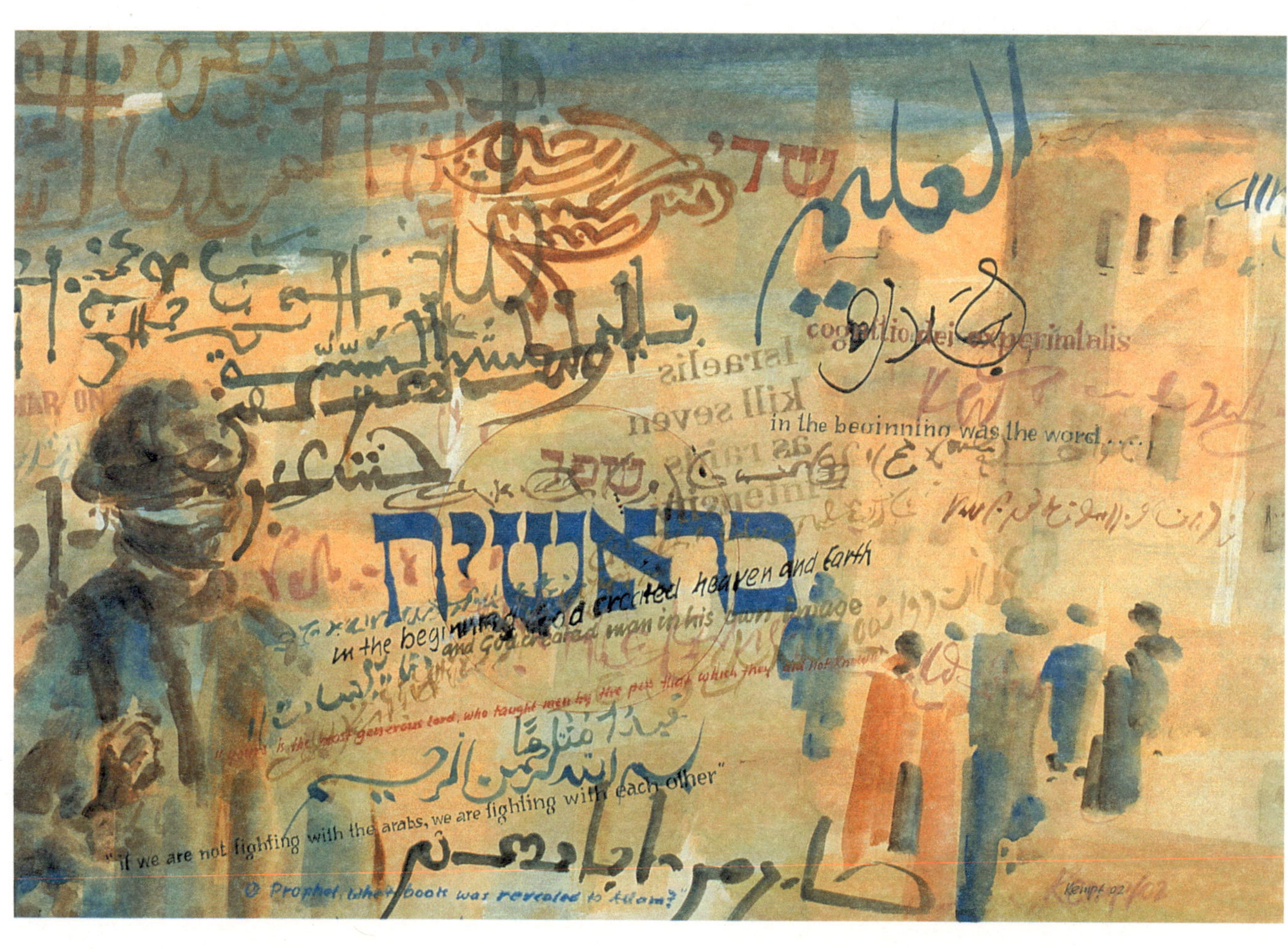

In the Beginning, 2002, watercolour, 45.5 x 64.5

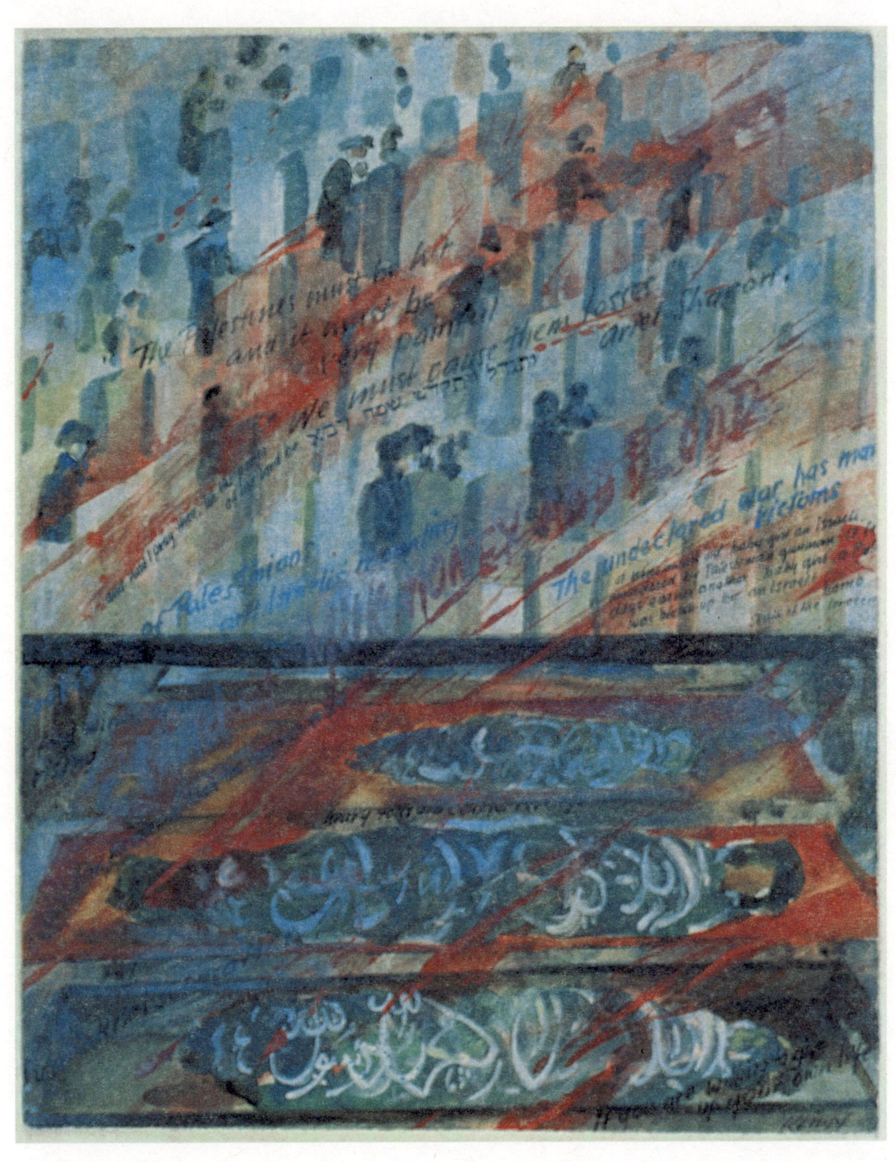

Lamentations II, 2002, mixed media on paper, 53 x 41

FRANZ KEMPF | CURRICULUM VITAE

CHRONOLOGY

1926 Born in Melbourne

1942 School of Art, Prahran Technical College

1944–45 Swinburne College of Technology

1946–47 National Gallery School, Melbourne

1950–56 Taught at various private schools

1955 Worked with Jessie Traill

1956 Peitro Vannuci Academy of Fine Art, Italy

1957 Worked with Oskar Kokoshka, Salzburg

1957 Frey & Kratz, Zurich

1957 Film Designer, Hallas and Bachelor, London

1958–59 Assistant to Creative Director TV, Dolan, Ducker, Whitcombe & Stewart, London

1960–61 Lecturer, Royal Melbourne Institute of Technology

1962 Lecturer, South Australian School of Art

1963 Associate of Industrial Design Institute of Australia

1964 Fellow, Royal Society of Arts – London

1964 Adelaide Festival of Arts poster

1969 Studied printmaking centres, Israel

1969 Etching for book cover *Mainly Modern,* Rigby Publishing, Adelaide

1969 Studied printmaking in Israel

1969 Members' Print for Print Council of Australia

1973 Appointed Senior Lecturer Printmaking, South Australian School of Art

1974 Edition of prints for University of Adelaide Centenary

1975 Studied print workshops in Israel and Europe

1976 Commissioned to write *Contemporary Australian Printmakers*, Lansdowne Editions, Melbourne

1977 Study tour, Tokyo–England–Paris

1978 Bodford Terrace folio print for Victorian Labor Party

1979 Guest Lecturer, Slade School of Fine Art, University of London

1981 Guest Lecturer, Edinburgh College of Art, Scotland

1981 Guest Lecturer, Gloucestershire College of Art, Cheltenham, United Kingdom

1981 Left South Australian School of Art to work full time in own studio – St Peters Editions, South Australia

1982 Series of lithographs for Hilton Hotel Adelaide

1982–83 Worked on series of paintings and prints centred in the Coorong

1984 Publication of *Franz Kempf – Graphic Works*, Neville Weston, Wakefield Press

1985 Returned to England, painted in East Anglia, worked in France and Israel

1986 Five paintings and six prints for Parliament House, Canberra

1987 Visited America, exhibiting twenty-two paintings and prints in Australia – *Different View*

1988 Returned to America, taking part in two exhibitions and an interview on CBS television. Invited as Artist-in-Residence to Mishkenot Sha'ananim, Jerusalem. Worked at Burston Graphic Centre, Jerusalem

1988–89 Returned to Australia, completed works for exhibition and produced a lithograph for fortieth anniversary of the State of Israel

1990 Worked with Craftman's Press on publication of book by Rosemary Brooks

1991 Launch of book, *Franz Kempf*, and retrospective exhibition of paintings

1991 Book cover for … *und der Alptraum wurde zum Alltag*, Certaurus, Germany

1992 Preparation of retrospective print exhibitions and new works

1993 Exhibited, Swan Hill Regional Art Gallery, Victoria, and McClelland Art Gallery, Langwarrin, Victoria

1993 Westpac Gallery – Victorian Arts Centre

Published article 'Ultimate Goal', *Generation Magazine*, Victoria

1995 The Jerusalem Tapestry/Victorian Tapestry Workshop

1995 Film, *The Franz Kempf Story*, Michael de Montignie

1996 Travelling Exhibition, Vic Arts, *The Wandering Jew, Myth and Metaphor*

1997 Exhibition *Paintings & Drawings*, BMG Art, Adelaide

1999 Book cover, *Sofala and other poems*, Kate Llewllyn, Hudson Publishing

2000 Exhibition *Paintings, Drawings*, BMG Art, Adelaide

2002 *Thinking on Paper*, 1955–2002, Flinders University Art Museum, Adelaide

MAJOR EXHIBITIONS

1953 Four-person exhibition, Collins Street Gallery, Melbourne

1964 Two-person exhibition, Museum of Modern Art, Melbourne

1965 Two-person exhibition, Hungry Horse Gallery, Sydney, paintings and prints

1966 Ben Uri Galleries, Melbourne, etchings, serigraphs and lithographs

One-person exhibition, Nundah Gallery, Canberra

1967 One-person exhibition, White Studio Exhibition Gallery, Adelaide

1968 Etchings and serigraphs, Llewellyn Galleries, Adelaide Festival, gouaches

One-person exhibition, Leveson Street Gallery, Melbourne, paintings and prints

1969 Etchings and serigraphs, The Zamel Prize Exhibition, The Gallery, Adelaide

1971 Paintings and prints, Derek Hunt Gallery, Perth Festival

1972 One-person exhibition, Llewellyn Galleries, Adelaide Festival

1984 Paintings and prints, 1962–1984, Tynte Gallery, Adelaide

1986 Publication of eight works reproduced on postcards

Recent monotypes, Tynte Gallery, Adelaide

1988 Works on paper, Zantman Galleries, Mariot Springs Hotel, Palm Springs, California

1989 Paintings, pastels and monotypes, Kensington Gallery, Adelaide

1991 *Paintings 1955–1990*, Nodrum Gallery, Melbourne

Paintings 1955–1990, Adelaide Town Hall Function Centre

1992 *Franz Kempf, The Painter as Printmaker,* Mildura Art Centre Gallery, Mildura, and McClelland Gallery, Langwarrin

1993 *Franz Kempf, The Painter as Printmaker,* Swan Hill Regional Art Gallery, Swan Hill, and McClelland Gallery, Langwarrin

1994 *Franz Kempf Recent Work,* BMG Art, Adelaide

1995 *Franz Kempf Recent Work,* Flinders Lane Gallery, Melbourne

1997 *Paintings & Drawings,* BMG Art, Adelaide

2000 *Franz Kempf Recent Work,* BMG Art, Adelaide

2002 *Thinking on Paper 1956–2002,* Flinders University Art Museum, Adelaide

SELECTED GROUP EXHIBITIONS

1963 *Australian Print Survey*, Art Gallery of New South Wales, all states

South Australian Graphic Arts Society, David Jones' Gallery, Adelaide

1964 *South Australian Graphic Arts Society*, David Jones' Gallery, Adelaide

Cornell Prize Exhibition, Contemporary Art Society, Adelaide

1965 *Contemporary Israeli Graphic Art*, Jewish Museum of Art, travelling exhibition

1966 *Australian Prints*, Smithsonian Institution, Washington DC, USA

Australian Printmaking Today, Contemporary Art Society, Adelaide Festival

Contemporary Australian Drawing, Newcastle City Art Gallery

Newcastle Contemporary Art Society Annual Interstate Exhibition, Blaxland Gallery, Sydney

1967 *Mirror-Warratah Festival Graphic Prize Exhibition*, Sydney

Interstate Exhibition, Contemporary Art Society of Australia, Newcastle Region Art Gallery, Newcastle

Print Prize Exhibition, Print Council of Australia, all states

1968 *Printmakers*, National Gallery of Victoria, Melbourne

Survey '68, White Studio Exhibition Gallery, Adelaide

1969 *Georges Invitation Prize*, Melbourne Toorak Art Gallery, Melbourne

Third Print Prize Exhibition, Print Council of Australia, all states

1970 *The Australian-TAA National Art Award*, travelling exhibition

Collection Elliot Aldridge Post-War Paintings, South Australian School of Art, Adelaide

1971 *Australian Imprint*, National Gallery of Victoria, Kuala Lumpur, Department of Foreign Affairs

International Biennale Print Exhibition, Print Council of Australia, Cracow, Poland

1972 *Australian Printmakers*, Pratt Graphics Centre, New York

British International Print Biennale Jewish Artists in Australia 1812–1972, Sculpture Centre, Sydney

The Alice Prize, Alice Springs Art Foundation, Alice Springs

1973 *Australian Prints*, Australian Council of Victoria, Melbourne

Caltex Festival of Drawing, Mornington Peninsula, Victoria

Wspolczesna Grafika Australiijska, Cracow, Poland

1974 *Recent Art from South Australia*, Contemporary Art Society, Adelaide and Newcastle City Art Gallery, Newcastle

Australian Prints on Tour, Arts Council of Australia, travelling exhibition

1975 *Twelve Australian Lithographers*, Print Council of Australia, travelling exhibition

1976 *Artists of Adelaide*, Adelaide Fine Art and Graphics, Adelaide

Thinking on Paper, Invitation Drawing Exhibition, Contemporary Art Society, Adelaide

1977 *Art Purchase Exhibition*, Blue Gum Festival, Tasmanian Museum and Art Gallery, Tasmania

45th Exhibitions of the Japan Print Association, Tokyo, travelling exhibition

Contemporary Australian Prints, Western Australian Art Gallery, Perth Festival, Perth

Third Independent Exhibition of Prints, Print Council of Australia, Kanagawa, Japan

Contemporary Australian Prints, Studio Graphics, Sydney

1980 *Selections of a Century*, Art Gallery of South Australia, Adelaide

Painting in South Australia Today, Art Gallery of South Australia, Adelaide

Australian Art in Prints 1970–1980, Queen Victoria Museum, Launceston

1981 *Original Prints in Secondary School*, Education Department of Victoria, Melbourne

Painting in South Australia Today, Art Gallery of South Australia, Adelaide

Selections of a Century, Art Gallery of South Australia, Adelaide

The John McCaughey Memorial Prize, National Gallery of Victoria, Melbourne

Graven Images in the Promised Land, Art Gallery of South Australia, Adelaide

1982 *South Australian Printmakers*, Royal South Australian Society of Arts, Adelaide

South Australian Artists, State Branch, Australian Labor Party, Adelaide

The Australian Landscape, Tynte Gallery, Adelaide

The Holocaust Exhibition, University of Adelaide

1983 *New England Regional Art Museum*, Armidale, New South Wales

Artists in St Peters, Experimental Art Foundation, Adelaide

1984 *Mini Prints*, Print Council of Australia, Melbourne

New Works by Gallery Artists, Tynte Gallery, Adelaide

1987 *Australia: A Different Vision*, Landell Studios, Carmel, California, USA

Australian Art Collection, Zantman Galleries, Palm Desert, California

Collectors' Christmas, Tynte Gallery, Adelaide

1988 *Paintings and Prints*, Zantman Galleries, Palm Springs, California, USA

Printmaking and Sculpture, Temple Beth Israel, Melbourne

Spring Exhibition, Kensington Gallery, Adelaide

Artists for Amnesty International, Hilton Hotel, Adelaide

Affordable Treasures, Kensington Gallery, Adelaide

1989 *Paintings and Prints of the 60s*, Allyn Fisher Fine Arts, Bendigo, New South Wales

More Affordable Treasures, Kensington Gallery, Adelaide

1990 *Homage to Vincent*, Vincent Art Gallery, Adelaide

Artists' View of the Female Nude, Kensington Gallery, Adelaide

1992 *Being Contemporary, 1942–1992*, Contemporary Art Society of South Australia, Adelaide

New Art Seven, Kensington Gallery, Adelaide

Henri Worland Memorial Print Award 1972–1992, Warnambool Art Gallery, Victoria

1993 *An Exhibition of Contemporary Art*, Jewish Festival Art, Westpac Gallery, Victorian Art Centre, Melbourne

1995 *The Wandering Jew: Myth and Metaphor*, Jewish Museum of Australia, Melbourne, and travelling exhibition 1995–1997

Mask Auction, Jewish Museum of Australia, Melbourne

1997 *The Forgotten Fifties to the Swinging Sixties*, Noel Stott Fine Art Gallery, Melbourne

1998 *We Are Australians*, Victorian Art Centre, travelling exhibition to all state and regional galleries

2001 *16th Asian International Art Exhibition*, Guandong, China

REPRESENTED BY PAINTINGS OR PRINTS IN THE FOLLOWING PUBLIC COLLECTIONS

Victoria and Albert Museum, London

Betsalel National Museum, Jerusalem

Mishkenot Sha'ananim, Jerusalem

Beit Hanassi, Jerusalem

The Jewish Museum of Australia, Melbourne

Exeter University, Exeter, United Kingdom

Australian National Gallery, Canberra

Art Gallery of South Australia, Adelaide

National Gallery of Victoria, Melbourne

Art Gallery of New South Wales, Sydney

Art Gallery of Western Australia, Perth

Geelong Art Gallery, Geelong

Mildura Arts Centre Gallery, Mildura

Newcastle Regional Art Gallery, Newcastle

Bendigo Art Gallery, Bendigo

Warrnambool Art Gallery, Warrnambool

Flinders University Art Museum, Adelaide

University of Adelaide, Adelaide

University of Tasmania, Hobart

University of Melbourne, Melbourne

Reserve Bank of Australia, Canberra

Broken Hill Proprietary House Collection, Broken Hill

Woolongong City Art Gallery, Woolongong

Swan Hill Gallery of Contemporary Art, Swan Hill

Premier's Department, New South Wales

University of South Australia, Adelaide

Wagga Wagga Art Gallery, Wagga Wagga

New England Regional Art Museum, Armidale

St Anns College, Adelaide

Queen Victoria Museum and Art Gallery, Launceston

Tasmanian Museum and Art Gallery, Hobart

Waite Agricultural Research Institute, Adelaide

Hilton International Hotel, Adelaide

Parliament House, Canberra

Australian National University, Canberra

Australian National Museum, Canberra

Guandong Museum of Art, China

SELECTED CATALOGUE ESSAYS AND REVIEWS

Ashkenazi, Susie, 'New Paintings by Franz Kempf', *Jewish News*, May 1995

Dutkiewicz, Adam, 'Reflections on Life's Journey', *Advertiser*, September 1997

Dutkiewicz, Adam, 'Romantic Landscape in the Abstract', *Advertiser*, December 1994

Emery, John, 'Kempf uncovered', *Advertiser*, May 1991

Grishin, Sasha, 'The Voyages of Franz Kempf', *Franz Kempf Recent Work*, BMG Art, Adelaide, 1997

Grishin, Sasha, 'Discord in Harmony', *Franz Kempf Recent Work*, BMG Art, Adelaide, 1994

Grishin, Dr Sasha, 'Discord in Harmony', *Franz Kempf Recent Work*, Flinders Lane Gallery, Melbourne, 1995

Grishin, Sasha, 'Franz Kempf Works on Paper', Flinders University Art Museum, 2002

Harris, Samela, 'Outsiders and Witnesses in Art', *Advertiser*, September 1995

Jawary, Anita, 'Insights into a Creative Life', *Australian Jewish News*, Melbourne edition, November 1992

de Jong-Duldig, Eva, 'Printmaker Presents a Fascinating Look at Life', *Arts/Review*, April 1993

Kronenberg, Simon, 'An Exhibition of Contemporary Art', *Jewish Festival of Art*, Westpac Gallery, Victorian Art Centre, Melbourne, 1993

Larkin, John, 'Return of a Graduate from the Academy of Free Spirit', *Melbourne Age*, May 1995

Larkin, John, 'The View from Within and Above', *Franz Kempf Recent Work*, BMG Art, 2000

Lloyd, Tim, 'Abstract Meets Landscape', *Advertiser*, December 1994

McDonald, Katherine, 'Henri Worland Print Award, 1972–1992', Warrnambool Art Gallery, Victoria

Neylon, John, 'Most Documented Living', *Adelaide Review*, 1991

Smith, Dr Ernest and Smith, Robert, 'Franz Kempf The Painter as Printmaker 1955–1992', Mildura Art Gallery, Swan Hill Regional Gallery, McClelland Gallery, Langwarrin

SELECTED BIBLIOGRAPHY

Benko, Nancy, *Art and Artists of South Australia*, Lidums, Adelaide, 1969

Berger, George, *Franz Kempf*, Brolga, Adelaide, 1969

Bonython, Kym, *Modern Australia Painting 1970–1975*, Rigby, Adelaide, 1976

Brook, Donald, *Franz Kempf: Paintings, Pastels and Prints*, Kensington Gallery, Adelaide, 1989

Brooks, Rosemary, foreword by Thomson, Gordon, *Franz Kempf*, Craftsman House, Sydney, 1991

Campbell, Jean, *Australian Watercolour Painters, 1780 to the Present Day*, Craftsman House, Sydney, 1989

Dolan, David, 'Franz Kempf', *Art and Australia*, Vol 14, No 1, July–September 1976

Dolan, David, 'Franz Kempf', *Imprint* No 1, Print Council of Australia, Melbourne, 1975

Drury, Nevill, *Images in Contemporary Australian Painting*, Craftsman House, Sydney, 1992, 1993, 1994

Drury, Nevill, *New Art 7*, Craftsman House Press, Sydney, 1992

Encyclopaedia Judaica, Keter, Jerusalem, 1971

Grishin, Sasha, *Contemporary Australian Printmaking*, Craftsman House, Sydney, 1994

Hoff, Ursula, *Franz Kempf: Etchings, Serigraphs and Lithographs*, Ben Uri Galleries, Melbourne, 1965

Luck, Ross, *A Guide to Modern Australian Painting*, Sun Books, Melbourne, 1969

McCulloch, Alan, *Encyclopedia of Australia Art*, Macmillan Melbourne, 1969

Newman, Thelma R., *Innovative Printmaking*, Crown Publishers Inc., New York, 1997

Smith, Bernard, *Australian Painting 1788–1970*, 2nd edition, Oxford University Press, Melbourne, 1971

Thomson, Gordon, *Franz Kempf: Paintings and Prints*, Tynte Gallery, Adelaide, 1984

Weston, Neville, *Franz Kempf: Graphic Works 1962–1984*, Wakefield Press, Adelaide, 1984